MANAGING PEOPLE

Recruiting and Retaining Staff in Private Practice

Matthew Moore LLB, Solicitor
and
Martin Moore BSc(Econ), Grad IPM

Chancery Law Publishing
London

MANAGING LAWYERS
Recruiting and Retaining Staff in Private Practice

MATTHEW MOORE graduated in law as an external student of London University in 1975, having attended what is now the Anglia Higher Education College in Chelmsford. He then taught law for several years at colleges in Essex and Devon before serving articles and practising as a solicitor in Coventry. In 1985 he became the first employee of the then M5 group, subsequently developing various recruitment initiatives with the group for trainee and admitted staff. He is now a management consultant advising firms on marketing, training and human resources issues.

Other publications: *The Law and Procedure of Meetings* (Sweet & Maxwell) 1979; *Marketing for Lawyers* (Law Society Gazette Practice Handbooks) 1990.

MARTIN MOORE was educated at University College, Cardiff and Washington State University. He first worked in personnel management with Shell UK, gaining experience in both its distribution and North Sea operations. His subsequent experience encompasses electronics manufacturing and the retail distribution industry. He is currently an employee relations manager at the Hatfield site of British Aerospace (Commercial Aircraft) Ltd.

Published in the United Kingdom 1991 by
Chancery Law Publishing Ltd,
Baffins Lane, Chichester,
West Sussex PO19 1UD
National Chichester (0243) 779777
International +44 243 779777

Reprinted March 1994

Typeset by Florencetype Ltd
Kewstoke, Avon

Printed by Antony Rowe Ltd,
Chippenham, Wiltshire

Design by Fielding Rowinski

ISBN 0-471-93669-3

All rights reserved. No part of this publication
may be reproduced in any form or by any means, electronic,
mechanical, photocopying, recoding or otherwise, or stored in any
retrieval system without the written permission of
the copyright holders and the publishers.

M Moore and M Moore

Contents

Acknowledgements viii
Preface ix

1 Planning and Policies 1
   The Human Resources Plan 2
   An Integrated Approach 4
   Personnel Policies 7
   Summary 9

2 Job Analysis 10
   The Objectives of Analysis 11
   The Process of Analysis 13
   Job Descriptions 14
   Person Specifications 16
   Summary 18

3 The Candidates 19
   Admitted Staff 19
   Trainee Solicitors 23
   Secretaries 25
   Legal Executives 26

4 Attracting the Candidates 28
   Existing Staff 29
   Former Staff 29
   Recommendations 30
   Previous Applicants 31
   Recruitment Agencies 31
   Selection Consultants 32
   Search Consultants 33
   Advertising 33

5 Selection Interviewing — 39
Interviewing — 41
Interview Checklist — 45
Case Study — 46

6 Psychological Testing — 48
Testing's Potential — 48
Choosing Tests — 52
Factors for and against — 54
Summary — 55

7 Offer and Acceptance — 56
References — 57
Medical Examination — 61
Legal Formalities — 62
Maintaining Contact — 64

8 Induction — 66
Contents of Induction Programmes — 67
The Psychological Challenge — 70
Mentoring — 73
The Training Input — 74
Case Study — 74
Summary — 75

9 Employment Records — 77
Areas requiring Records — 77
Form of Records — 80
The Data Protection Act 1984 — 82
Confidentiality — 84

10 Appraisal — 85
Objectives — 86
Developing an Appraisal Scheme — 88
The Interview — 90
Pitfalls and Dangers — 92
Summary — 93

11 Employment Problems	94
Rules and Procedures	94
Disciplinary Interviews	98
Grievances	101
Appeals	102
Summary	103

Appendix A
Recruitment Consultancies and Agencies
specialising in legal staff   105

Appendix B
Institutions offering law degrees in England
and Wales   112

Appendix C
Code of Practice for the Recruitment of
Trainee Solicitors   120

Index   123

Acknowledgements

Stephen Harwood	The Law Society
John Hamilton	John Hamilton Associates, Guildford
Rosemary Hill	Law Department, Bristol Polytechnic
Mark Jeffries	Mills & Reeve
Fiona O'Kane	Trainee Solicitors Group
Margaret Mannell	Taylor Joynson Garrett
Charlotte Points	Mills & Reeve
Brian Read	Careers Department, Sheffield University
Jane Reynolds	The Law Society
Bob Scott	Middle Management Resources, Birmingham
Jayne Willetts	Young Solicitors Group
Sally Woodward	Freshfields
John Young	Denton Hall Burgin & Warrens

The Law Society Gazette for permission to use a joint article previously appearing in the *Gazette* as the basis of Chapter 5.

The partners of the firm providing the management calculation appearing at the start of Chapter 5.

Price Waterhouse for the report referred to in Chapter 4.

Preface

All firms rightly regard the responsibility of managing their staff as being a crucial element of practice management. There are, as such, no physical products involved in the supply of legal services, only people. It follows that effective management of lawyers is an important contributing factor in maintaining an efficient service for clients and is also a vital component for successful practice development.

As in other aspects of practice management there is a great deal to learn from studying practices adopted elsewhere. Our aim has been to harness the experience that one of us has as a personnel professional in a range of industrial environments, and the experience of the other gained as a solicitor in private practice, and subsequently in practice management. In the few situations where standard personnel practice does not seem to us to convert to the reality of private practice, pragmatism has prevailed. We have set out to produce an entirely practical handbook which will be directly relevant to the requirements of firms of all types and sizes.

The book is aimed at all partners who find themselves with the responsibility of managing staff, notwithstanding the lack of management training which solicitors have long suffered from. We also hope that the book will be useful for the increasing numbers of personnel professionals who are taking up positions in solicitors' firms. For these readers in particular the rules may be familiar, but the context different; acclimatising to the special circumstances of law firm management can sometimes be a source of difficulty.

In technical terms we have set out to concentrate on the resourcing and retention issues facing legal firms. This means that other important areas of personnel management have not been covered, but further titles in this new series will explore these areas further. We are delighted to be the authors of the first book to be published by Chancery Law Publishing and our thanks are due to Andrew, Jane and all their staff. We wish them every future success.

Our thanks are also due to the contributors who have provided case studies which make their points better than we could have done, and also to the other firms and individuals who have consented to being quoted in the text. Our older brother Michael, a personnel manager in the Midlands, kindly provided some useful materials for our research. This means that it would be invidious not to mention our other brother Mark, a lecturer at the Polytechnic of North London, and our parents. The major personal thanks and acknowledgement, however, must go to our wives, Angela and Nicola and to Matthew's daughter, Eleanor.

MATTHEW MOORE
MARTIN MOORE
December 1990

Chapter 1
Planning and Policies

Private practice lends itself to short-termism. Such are the myriad demands for attention from clients that few lawyers can plan their days in advance with absolute confidence, and much of the daily activities of any given partnership will consist of 'fire-fighting' on a number of different fronts. Developing a pro-active role, and taking the initiative to clients, is all well and good, but in the final analysis clients instruct their legal advisers, and it is the advisers who have to respond to the demands made of them.

Solicitors should not feel that they are alone in suffering from what often seems to be a haphazard working routine. Such surveys which have been conducted into the real activities of managers tend to uncover results that may well sound familiar to the busy practitioner.

> Research into the activities of nine Swedish managing directors revealed that they worked long hours ($8\frac{1}{2}$–11 hours per day), but tended to be surprised by these results when they were made aware of them and consistently thought that the period under inspection was unrepresentative. As a group they realised that their work patterns were unsatisfactory and they criticised themselves for neglecting policy, which in turn meant that they spent too much time dealing with one-off decisions. (Sune Carlson)

This latter point – that the volume of individual decisions to be made increases if policy is neglected – was termed 'administrative pathology' by Carlson. The idea has been taken up and supported by later British writers in conducting similar research into manufacturing industries in this country, where it has been found to be very much in evidence (Hutton and Lawrence, 1982).

Here, then, is the major reason for taking the time to develop and implement a human resources plan, and a number of employment policies. The plan will predict the level of activity which will be needed to maintain and develop a satisfactory workforce. The employment policies will lay down plans and guidelines for a number of recurring situations, such as maternity absence and staff health problems. Plans and policies provide improved prospects of consistency of decision making, and a sense of direction in recruitment and personnel matters. They will serve to reduce the 'administrative pathology' which solicitors, like their management counterparts, often recognise to be be a problem.

It is possible to regard the contents of a book on personnel management which concentrates on issues of recruitment and retention as being in the main advice on the countless decisions which the partners and other managers are called upon to make. The adoption of a human resources plan and a number of policies to support it will simplify the process, and will therefore allow more time for the core activity of partners in legal firms – handling instructions for clients in order to make a profit.

The Human Resources Plan

At its simplest level the human resources plan will predict the likely numbers of people that the firm will need to recruit over the period of the plan, and will make provisions for how the supply will be maintained. There may well be conclusions on the implications of these main findings, such as the improvements that will be needed to the firm's training programme, career structure or other such matters. As with all aspects of practice management planning, the firm will benefit from taking control of what amounts to a fundamental business activity. Armed with their human resources plan the partners are likely to conclude that there is more to recruitment than merely filling vacancies as they arise, with little notion of the budgetary consequences of doing so. The sense of direction gained by adopting a plan should also increase the prospects of selecting appropriate individuals for the practice, thereby reducing the risks of expensive errors.

The main steps in preparing a plan are as follows:

1. conduct an internal staff audit;
2. assess patterns of resignations and retirements;
3. determine the required rate of practice growth;
4. calculate the recruitment needs;
5. describe factors affecting the desired recruitment rate;
6. state conclusions on relevant implications.

1. **Internal audit**

An assessment of the current personnel of the firm is the obvious starting point for the planning exercise. Details should be drawn up on the current numbers of partners, solicitors and other members of staff, showing the age and seniority of all involved.

2. **Resignations and retirements**

The pattern of resignations over the previous 12 months is the best clue to the likely trend over the year to come, and in the absence of exceptional circumstances should prove to be a reasonably accurate prediction of what the partners might expect. Retirements are easier to predict.

3. **Rate of growth**

It is now necessary to examine the business plan of the firm to see what rate of growth is planned. The business plan can be the substantial document preferred by some, or can be a short and simple statement of the overall philosophy and aims of the partnership. Whatever its shape and contents some thought and attention will need to have been given to the development of the practice in order for human resources planning to be possible

4. Calculate recruitment needs

It should now be possible to perform a simple recruitment calculation, using very basic arithmetic:

Recruitment Demand =
Projected Requirements − Adjusted Staff Figures.

5. Factors affecting supply

The major factor which all types of employers are having to give consideration to at present is the so-called 'demographic trough' which will be at its most aggravated in the middle of the current decade (see page 26). Other local factors might also be relevant, in which case they should be thrown into the planning process at this stage.

6. Conclusions and implications

Conclusions on how the firm can make itself more attractive as an employer to the various classes of employees that it requires should be set out for discussion and approval by the partnership. One of the most important conclusions to be drawn will be the cost of implementing the plan and a budget should be put forward for consideration by the partners.

An Integrated Approach

The rather mechanical approach to human resources planning set out above will prove an extremely worthwhile exercise for firms of all types and sizes. Within the process of drawing up the plan the partners may be confronted with some wider issues that require attention, perhaps the need to admit greater numbers than usual to partnership in order to retain senior assistants who might otherwise seek partnerships elsewhere. A problem considered and addressed in advance is often a problem which can be avoided altogether, if there is the resolve on the part of the partners to deal with the issue.

It can be argued, however, that human resources planning could and should be taken much further. If human resources planning is extended into human resources development it might even become the principal strategy for achieving the practice development goals of the firm. Beyond what might be termed a 'structural approach' to human resources management, in which an organised approach to recruitment contributes to the overall efficiency of the practice, it is possible to adopt a 'dynamic' approach in which the area of human resources is used as a means to effect change within the firm. Human resources management might even be used to change the ethos or culture of the firm, and to confer these values on the staff within the practice.

Exploiting the full potential of human resources management within a legal firm should be an attractive proposition to those with responsibility for managing the practice. If asked what it is that distinguishes them from their rivals, most solicitor's firms will reply that it is the quality of service that they offer to clients. Often partners will be indulging in wishful thinking in describing the excellence of their service, realising that there are in fact deficiencies which have the effect of stifling further profitable development. Whatever the present situation in any given firm, there is likely to be agreement that improving the quality of service to clients will hold the key to planned practice development. How then, should an improved service be developed?

Marketing plays an important role in identifying the clients that the firm should concentrate on and by investigating their requirements. This information can be used to instigate improvements where necessary, and to revise existing services so that they are more attractive to identifiable client groups. Publicity can be used to inform clients and intermediaries of the range and quality of services which are available. Marketing, however, is simply a means of discovering opportunities, and then describing and creating the means for those opportunities to be exploited. It is the partners and staff who hold the key to achieving an improved service. Human resources management has the potential to define improvements which are needed to existing staff and can also provide for improved standards in the selection of new staff. An integrated approach to practice management is required in which excellence is the goal and in which personnel management is seen as one of the prime means to achieve it, along with all related areas of practice management.

There are two main implications to approaching human resources management in this integrated way:

1. The individual within the firm becomes much more the focus of management attention than traditional organisational objectives. An alternative way of looking at this is that management becomes much more a matter of getting the best from the people within the firm than using these people to achieve predetermined performance goals.
2. The separate management and administrative functions that fall to different partners or managers within the practice must be regarded as different aspects of the same policy, rather than separate and autonomous policies altogether.

Within this integrated approach to practice management there is a great deal to be said for developing an overall business plan for the period deemed appropriate by the partners, and then producing an integrated implementation plan annually which will define the steps that are needed to succeed in the overall objectives. In addition to the traditional assessment of recruitment needs a human resources plan should therefore go on to define how the personnel management within the practice can work with other key elements of practice management, in order to achieve the objectives determined by the partners. The implementation plan may mean that there is no separate document as such entitled 'the human resources plan'; what matters more is that human resources management and planning plays its proper pivotal role in the profitable development of the practice.

Personnel Policies

The partners should consider how many areas would benefit from having a policy to communicate the attitude of the partners to decisions which will need to be made. Formulating the policy will have an immediate benefit in directing the attention of the partners to issues where a common line will be important, and the policy adopted will form a clear indication to employees of how decisions will be made on a variety of relevant issues.

Policies should ideally form part of a cohesive approach to personnel management within the firm and should therefore be seen to support each other. This is turn will mean that policies should not be merely circulated to the staff as yet further office memoranda, but should form part of a comprehensive guide to work in the practice. The office manual is the ideal way in which to achieve this approach and although it can be a highly time-consuming task, partnerships should regard the development of a manual as time well spent. Harassed partners or managers facing what seems to be the impossible task of collating all this information are likely to find the sample manual prepared by the Law Society, and available from Law Society Publications, extremely helpful. (*The Law Society Solicitors Office Manual*, Stephen Hammett)

A typical firm might adopt policy statements in respect of the following topics:

- Recruitment and selection
- Career structures and training

- Maternity absence and payments; returning to work after the birth and career breaks
- Grievance and disciplinary procedures
- Health and Safety at Work
- Employee health
- Pay and conditions of employment
- Client care
- Equal opportunities.

There could easily be many others, but within these headings fall most of the contentious issues which confront partnerships from time to time. What is the attitude of the firm to unpaid leave, smoking and alcohol in the offices, training opportunities in respect of the Institute of Legal Executives, use of the telephone for personal calls etc? The partner's role as a manager becomes the easier if a framework is laid down for all the decisions which need to be made and if the employees are given clear guidance on what amounts to acceptable behaviour.

The Health and Safety at Work policy is worthy of special mention as being a policy which the majority of firms must possess. The Health and Safety at Work Act 1974, requires all employers to have a written policy, except in firms employing fewer than five employees. Although legal offices might not have the potentially hazardous processes often seen in manufacturing industries, there are risks in offices which should be carefully considered. A publication from the Health and Safety Executive entitled 'Writing your Health and Safety Policy: Our Health and Safety Policy Statement: Guide to Preparing a Safety Policy Statement for a Small Business' is recommended for those setting about the task. It is available from HMSO at a moderate charge. Also available is a short leaflet 'Writing a Safety Policy Statement – Advice to Employers' which is free of charge.

Finally, the importance of observing policies once they are adopted should be emphasised. All the policies of the firm will soon fall into disrepute if the partners ignore their provisions in all but the clearly exceptional cases. Living by the codes is more important than adopting them in the first place, and consistency of decision making is the improvement that policies offer. Fine words which have been agreed in abstract must be taken through and put into practice.

Summary

A human resources plan will provide the partnership with a sense of purpose and direction in its recruitment activities and in other aspects of practice management. The overriding importance of a committed and competent staff in the provision of professional services should be recognised, and human resources planning should be taken further than the process of maintaining satisfactory numbers and should be regarded as being a major aspect of practice development plans.

Employment policies serve to develop and communicate clear principles on aspects of personnel management within the practice. Policies should form part of a comprehensive approach by the partners towards personnel issues and it is important that the policies are implemented and referred to in all specific decisions which need to be made.

Chapter 2
Job Analysis

Job analysis is the process of examining a position in the firm in detail, usually before an appointment is made. It consists of collecting and processing information about the tasks, responsibilities and contexts of openings within the firm in order to create an objective statement of what is expected of the incumbent. Armed with the 'job description' which results from the process of analysis, the partners will be in a better position to make an informed and objective decision about the type of candidates it should be seeking. The resulting 'person specification' therefore emerges directly from the initial job description and can be said to be dependent upon it for its success.

The job description is fundamental to many of the other activities described in this book – selection of staff and employee induction chief amongst them. It therefore seems regrettable to note at the outset that job descriptions are more often than not conspicuous by their absence from private practice. One reason for this is that solicitors – in common with most other professionals – have their own detailed classification system for fee earning staff. This system is seen in the job advertisements which appear each week in relevant newspapers and journals, perhaps announcing openings for a 'Planning lawyer 2/3 years admitted' at one firm, or a 'Company commercial partner designate' at another. All such advertisements are likely to convey to readers with surprising accuracy the requirements of the practice in terms of applicants' technical competence and legal experience. Likewise, the view might be taken that an announcement of an opening for an 'experienced conveyancing secretary' in the local newspaper may be felt to be broadly sufficient in terms of initial job planning.

A further term requiring definition in this area is 'job evaluation'. This involves the analysis of the elements of any given job to produce a rating by which the job in question can be compared to others within the organisation. The purpose of job evaluation is usually to determine appropriate salary levels in organisations which employ specialists from a number of different backgrounds. It follows that job evaluation is of relatively little significance in the legal profession, although it is sometimes of concern in larger firms employing considerable numbers of expert administrative staff.

What part, then, do job descriptions and person specifications play in private practice; can they safely be ignored by the busy practitioner? Are they one of the important functions of personnel management in industry which do not necessarily convert to the legal profession? If, on the other hand, it transpires that they do serve a useful purpose, how should they be prepared?

The Objectives of Analysis

It is possible to regard the benefits of analysis from two different, but complementary, standpoints. First, the process is useful in a number of regards to the partnership itself, in:

- determining the actual level of employee required to perform identified tasks;
- obtaining agreement within the firm on the precise duties to be undertaken by the appointee;
- providing those involved with the selection of staff with clear criteria on which to base recruitment decisions;
- focusing attention on job differentials with regard to issues of salary administration;

- collecting objective data for human resources planning;
- adopting an agreed statement of priorities and standards for the new employees to be inducted and, subsequently, for their performance to be evaluated by.

Job analysis also works directly to the benefit of potential employees. The success of any position in a firm is not only a matter of the efforts of the individual concerned, but is also tied up with all the other factors of supporting relationships and the provision of a steady and realistic supply of work by the partners. In conducting job analysis the firm will improve the prospects of the employee being placed into a role where he or she is more likely to succeed, not only because the duties will be better defined, but also because the partners will have given attention to the attributes which will be needed by employees in that particular role.

One of the most useful functions of job analysis is to cause the partnership to question assumptions that might be held about the level of employee required for any given opening. The evidence collected in the first part of a job analysis exercise might lead the partners to conclude that an admitted solicitor is not in fact needed to perform a role which has been identified within the firm, with the result that economy can be achieved by the deployment of an able, and perhaps experienced, legal executive. In such situations the employee will benefit from the opportunity given to him or her, while a more highly qualified individual might be spared the frustration of having to cope with a job which does not present sufficient incentives for career development.

It is therefore fair to say that there is a shared interest between the partners and employees in job analysis being conducted and in the information being processed in an intelligible and communicable form. By ensuring that all applicants have a clear view of what the job actually entails the prospects of the appointment proving to be successful are enhanced; from the individual's point of view this also means that the dangers of career disruption are minimised.

The Process of Analysis

There are two basic stages to a job analysis exercise:

1. collection of information
2. formulation of recommendations and details into
   - job description, and
   - person specification

If analysis is required because a replacement will have to be found for a departing employee a useful starting point is to conduct an 'exit interview' with the leaver. Particular points which should be covered include:

- Was the job rewarding? If not, is it because the individual was misplaced or does the job need changing?
- Was there sufficient training to do the job properly?
- Was the supervision sufficient, excessive or inadequate?
- Were the career prospects attractive and well defined?
- How does the individual feel that the job should be changed to improve it for his or her successor?

How the exit interview should be conducted is largely a matter of style; some conduct formal interviews while others prefer an informal or even a casual conversation. It is important, however, that it is conducted by someone not directly associated with the work of the fee earner, since the interviewee should feel free to be able to comment on the activities and attitudes of the departmental partners.

All too often partners are content to explain the departure of a fee earner in terms that he or she wanted partner status which was more likely to be achieved elsewhere. The truth may well be very much more complex, but unless pressed on the point the departing employee is likely to offer a simple and uncontroversial justification for his or her decision to leave. The exit interview might not provide a completely unbiased perspective of the job or firm as the individual is likely to 'post-rationalise' his or her reasons for leaving, but a failure to conduct the exit interview probably represents a wasted opportunity to collect pertinent and useful information.

At this stage the discussions can be broadened, and the personnel manager or partner should talk to the other individuals who will be involved with the position to be filled. It is probably advisable that these interviews are semi-structured and may well develop points to emerge from the initial interview with the departing employee. Other methods of collecting information include requiring the present incumbent to complete a diary or 'log' of activities, but these can be highly time-consuming for the individual concerned.

Job Descriptions

There are a number of techniques for analysing the information once it has been collected, but the creation of a job description is usually regarded as the first main step. The traditional job description sets out relevant findings and conclusions under the following broad headings:

- job title and other basic information such as the firm and its location;
- relationships with others: reporting relationships, other close working relationships, staff reporting to the job holder, departmental details;
- performance duties: main objectives and key tasks.

All this, of course, is essential information for the firm to convey to any new staff, but it must be a matter of judgement in each case how the objectives of providing this information can best be achieved. It may well be that an outline job description is a highly convenient way in which to record most of the information, but a detailed exposition might not be merited. If the partners do choose to dispense with job

Job Analysis

descriptions altogether, or if important details are omitted, it is important that they are communicated in some other way and ideally are recorded in writing. In one instance a provincial firm was seeking to appoint a company commercial solicitor from a City practice and was concerned that the individual might not understand the level of work that he would be expected to undertake. Time was therefore set aside after the interview for one of the partners to look through a number of typical files with the applicant. In this way it was felt that the dangers of misunderstanding by the applicant as to the quality of work would be minimised.

Preparing job descriptions is a task that lawyers should find easy to master, since the key to success is precise drafting of researched situations. The good job description is comprehensive but concise and is likely to draw a distinction between the main purpose of the position and the key tasks which will be involved in it. It is advisable to introduce the key tasks in a number of verbs: co-ordinating, supervising, managing etc. The main job description will usually be accompanied by a brief person specification.

It is tempting in a book on personnel management to regard job descriptions as being de facto a 'good thing'. What matters most, however, is that the objectives which lie behind job descriptions are met by the practice, in which case the method by which these objectives are attained becomes a secondary issue. An outline job description will not take an undue time to prepare and will certainly form a useful summary of important points relating to the appointment. On the other hand it is unlikely that the myriad demands for legal services within a firm or department will be capable of being defined in writing with precision and there may even be dangers in attempting to do so. Ungerson (1983) uncovered a number of problems in respect of the appropriateness of job descriptions, including evidence that job descriptions tend to be inflexible and can therefore form an impediment to a dynamic and evolving organisation. The tendency for job descriptions to become out of date is a danger to be aware of, and suggests that not only should flexibility be worked into the contents of descriptions, but also that regular updating should occur.

The case for the adoption of comprehensive job descriptions for support staff is considerably more persuasive, although Ungerson discovered widespread misgivings about job descriptions for senior management in commerce and industry. Here a lengthy individual contract letter might be needed, perhaps in conjunction with the job description. In the usual case, however, the argument in favour of job descriptions for support staff centres on the wide differentials that might exist within the same job title in different firms. Do the partners look to a marketing manager to conduct all the firm's PR him or herself, for example, or is it envisaged that an external company will continue to be retained? Does policy formulation fall to the employee, or do the partners merely expect him or her to implement decisions that they have made? These are vital issues to consider if both sides wish to maximise the prospects of the appointment proving successful; failure to give proper attention to such questions may easily result in frustration for the partners and employee alike. A verdict on an employee that he or she was 'not really what we were looking for' is more often than not a tacit admission by the partners that they did not give sufficient consideration to what precisely they were looking for at the outset; job analysis and the development of job descriptions is the way in which to avoid a repetition of such problems.

Person Specifications

Having prepared the job description the partners will now be able to describe the qualities that will be needed for the appointee to succeed in the role. The person specification will clearly be highly relevant to the employee selection and will also serve to introduce objective criteria into what is otherwise likely to be an entirely subjective decision making process.

There are various devices for categorising personal attributes in the format of a person specification, John Munroe Fraser's five point framework and Alec Rodger's seven point plan chief amongst them.

Munroe Fraser	Rodger
1. Impact on others	Physical make-up
2. Qualifications or experience	Attainments
3. Brains and abilities	Intelligence
4. Motivation	Special aptitudes
5. Adjustment or balance	Interests
6.	Disposition
7.	Circumstances

There are clear advantages in using such a system to prepare a person specification and, in turn, in ensuring that it is used at the job interview in order to assess the candidate before the selection panel. Not only does the specification introduce objective criteria into the process, but it also encourages systematic consideration by the panel of all the interviewees and also introduces some guarantee that all the points felt to be of relevance will in fact be covered.

The most common error made by solicitors in compiling a person specification is the tendency to define the required candidate in unduly narrow terms, a fault which becomes all the more unfortunate if the person specification is subsequently used as the basis for a job advertisement and suitable candidates are thereby dissuaded from applying. Careful thought should be given to any requirement which will tend to restrict the pool of possible contenders, especially if they are in such areas as age or academic achievement where the potential for an individual to confound the characteristics of a stereotype should be recognised.

Summary

Job analysis should form an important role in the management of legal partnerships, although comprehensive job descriptions might not form the vital role in the process that they play elsewhere in respect of professional staff. If confusion could arise between employer and employee as to the precise nature of the position a carefully drafted job description is likely to prove invaluable.

The partners should consider each vacancy in detail in order that they can make reliable decisions as to what will be involved in the job in question and attention can also be given to the type of person required by the role. If careful research into these issues is conducted and appropriate conclusions are then developed and communicated to applicants, the prospects of securing and maintaining an effective and motivated workforce will be enhanced.

Chapter 3
The Candidates

A distinction is often made in private practice between fee earner and secretarial recruitment, with different individuals within the firm responsible for the two distinct groups of employees. Support staff might form a third group in larger firms, but even then tend to be recruited on a much more sporadic basis than their legal and secretarial colleagues.

Whereas industrialists need to maintain a wide band of specialisations to maintain their processes, solicitors in private practice are at an advantage in looking to recruit in the main from these two groups. This means that it is relatively easy to acquire an in-depth understanding of the relevant job markets. In this chapter we examine the main factors affecting the supply of candidates. No order of priority is suggested by the sequence in which we have dealt with the different types of employees.

Admitted Staff

First, a few facts and figures:

> There were 67,425 solicitors on the Roll at 31 July 1990; of these 54,734 held practising certificates. There were 10,272 solicitors' firms in 15,551 offices throughout England and Wales. There is a heavy concentration of solicitors working in London: 37% work there as opposed to the fact that 13.5% of the population live there. Even more remarkable is the fact that 42% of trainee solicitors commencing articles during 1989–90 did so in central London.

A total of 3,729 new solicitors were admitted to the Roll over the period 1 August 1989 to 31 July 1990, of whom 46.6% were women, 82% were graduates, and 67.3% were law graduates. The proportion of women solicitors continues to rise, 52% of trainees registering articles over the period of the survey being women.

So far as support staff are concerned there were approximately 46,000 solicitors, 28,000 other fee earners, and 100,000 administrative/support staff employed as at 31 March 1990.

(Source: Law Society Annual Statistical Report, 1990)

In the late 1980s the term 'recruitment crisis' became the great cliche of the legal profession. The supply of new staff and trainees fell behind employer demand in a time of rapidly increasing demand for legal services. The difficulty was not, as some suggested, in persuading enough suitable people to train to be solicitors; at all relevant times there was also excess demand for training places at the College of Law and Polytechnics. Unfortunately, there is an inbuilt delay between deciding to increase the supply of lawyers and their appearing on the job market since attendance on the Finals course is compulsory. Any shortage of legal staff is still mainly attributable to this training bottleneck, although the whole system is currently under review.

The new decade has seen a better balance struck between employers and potential candidates. Many firms are sufficiently resourced and are now filling isolated vacancies as they arise, or are seeking particular specialists in areas of targeted growth. The recruitment aspect of personnel management has become less frenetic, with many firms entering a period of consolidation following the spectacular growth of the previous five years. Unfortunately the general trend disguises numerous specific problems and many smaller general firms still experience considerable difficulty in recruiting legal staff, while commercial firms in London and the provinces still struggle to attract various types of specialists.

Legal recruitment agencies are often frustrated by client firms adopting an unduly narrow minded approach to fee earner recruitment. There are countless instances of able solicitors not being offered positions because they do not have the 'right blend of experience'. Litigators may be rejected because they have not done the right percentage of, say, employment law as opposed to insolvency law and much finer distinctions have often been seized upon by firms in rejecting otherwise promising applicants. Nonetheless, the same partners continue to complain of the difficulties of finding the right calibre of candidates. The problem appears to be the tendency of lawyers to concentrate too much on the past record of experience, and not enough on the candidate's future potential and aptitude to develop. This may well be a recruitment attitude borne of the lawyer's instinct to focus on details at the expense of wider issues.

The rapid increase in legal salaries over recent years has perhaps worked to the disadvantage of many candidates in this regard. According to one recent salary survey the average salary paid to a three year admitted commercial solicitor in London is £36,000 – a rate unlikely to be surpassed by many others in their late twenties. Salary rates may well mean that partners are justified in expecting new staff to be 'up and running' within a matter of days after joining the firm, let alone weeks or months.

Training, on the other hand, offers some hope of widening employers' parameters of expectation. As yet the tendency by most firms is still to approach training needs on a departmental rather than an individual basis, but further refinement to the excellent training systems which many firms have now established may well mean that more emphasis can be given to the needs of the individual employee.

These factors, coupled to a worrying trend of increased redundancies in the law, have inspired the Young Solicitors' Group to investigate a retraining initiative. This is linked to the redundancy helpline which was started some time ago, and which has revealed disturbing evidence of able professionals being made redundant simply because of a drop in demand for their particular specialisation. Those involved have all undergone the same examination system and are therefore technically able to practise any area of law; in reality abandoning one form of specialisation in favour of another is very much more difficult than it should be. The increased proportion of women entrants to the profession is often cited as a problem by legal recruiters, although it is difficult to view making the profession more representative of society as a whole as being anything other than beneficial. Nonetheless, certain personnel difficulties do arise which apply exclusively to female legal staff. It is unfortunate that critical decisions on partnership status tend to present themselves when most candidates are about the age of 30, coinciding for most women with other personal decisions about whether to have children. The permanent loss of women solicitors at this stage of their careers is a highly regrettable waste of valuable talent and the pool of female solicitors who have taken a break from full time working who would like to re-establish their careers should certainly be exploited. As always, a little imagination can be made to go a long way, and there is no reason why efforts cannot be made to keep the bond between a firm and its absent staff as, for example, by continuing to include them in the training programme and offering those involved occasional home-based tasks, thereby making an eventual return to the firm more likely.

A number of teaching institutions offer training courses to assist solicitors to re-orientate to legal practice after a break of a few years, and to enable others to retrain. One such is run by Bristol Polytechnic, who held their first course in September 1990:

> The five day course concentrated on substantive law and personal skills. Workshop sessions were held on changing management styles, CV preparation, interviewing techniques, and time management. The emphasis on practical issues was appreciated by delegates, who included a conveyancer who had been made redundant earlier in the year, who found a new position on the basis of attending the course. Other delegates included a number who had taken a career break to start a family. Confidence

building played an important part for all concerned, whatever their immediate career history.

Rosemary Hill: Course Tutor

Trainee Solicitors

Undergraduate recruitment by solicitors' firms has become something of a circus in recent years. Throwing any traditional conservatism to the wind solicitors' firms enter recruitment mode earlier than any other employer group. Interviews are held in the main at the start of the students' final year of degree studies or, in the case of non-law graduates, at the start of the Common Professional Examination conversion course. In the case of law and non-law applicants alike two important sets of examinations still have to be passed and a full two years at least will elapse before the successful candidates commence at the firm. Because of the prevailing examination structure lawyers would have good grounds to appear last on the University milk-round programme, but they are in fact the first. Undergraduates negotiate their examinations free of the worry of whether they will find a job (assuming of course that they have) and recruitment partners must hope that their estimate of future needs proves to be more or less correct.

Once the interviewing season is over, which in practice now means by late November, the next publicity season can commence. Faculties and departments throughout the land organise formal careers fairs and receptions which might occur in January at the earliest. The annual recruitment brochure is re-commissioned, the visual display boards are upgraded or dusted down and the roadshow is under way once more.

The rules by which this game is played come in differing degrees of formality: in practice everyone has a vested interest in abiding by them. First, and most informal, is the tendency of legal recruiters not to malign the opposition. Great offence is taken if the training at large, medium or small firms, in London or the provinces, is thrown into question by a member of a different group. Most prefer to be as polite as possible about the other firms on show and do no more than 'damn with faint praise'. This pays dividends in that the opposition are more likely to be nice about you and the candidates are bound to conclude that you are obviously eminently nice people to do business with.

Secondly, and still lacking in punitive enforcement, is the Law Society's Code for undergraduate recruiters (see Appendix C). The Code is currently under review and may well be changed into a new Guide during 1991. The main rule is that selection procedures may not occur before 1 September of the student's final year of degree studies. Transgressions seem mainly to occur when summer placement students find themselves in a firm before the start of their final year of degree studies. Promising candidates are told that there is no real need to apply elsewhere if they have enjoyed being at the firm. Nods and winks seem to play an important part in the student recruitment process at this stage.

A firm examining its undergraduate recruitment strategy might do well to consider two important factors. First is that law, which the majority of trainees will still have read, is a highly competitive subject to read at University, with entrance grades that are significantly higher than most other Arts and Social Sciences courses. Even the less popular Universities are likely to expect no less than two grade 'B's and one grade 'C' at 'A' level, which is indicative of good intellectual ability and sound application to study. Recruiting students from lesser known institutions is less of a risk in law than in other subjects. Likewise, the margin between 'A' level success and failure is very slight and a poor answer to just one or two questions on one 'A' level paper may result in the student being rejected by the University of his or her choice, but finding a place on a Polytechnic course. There are many highly able students in all law teaching institutions and recruiters are well advised to spread their nets more widely than just the traditional and better known Universities.

A further criticism of legal recruiters is that they often adopt an unfairly prejudicial attitude towards mature applicants for articles. Law is an attractive second career for many who are willing to undergo the privations of study later in life and many will not, contrary to rumour, fail to fit in with a training culture designed primarily to suit younger trainees. A frank conversation with one of the tutors to the mature student will reveal how well he or she mixed with younger students during degree studies and is likely to provide an accurate insight into how amenable the applicant will be to practical training in articles.

Appendix B consists of contacts and addresses of all the schools of law in England and Wales. It is difficult for firms to address potential CPE students before they enrol on their courses since they come from a much wider pool, but efforts to recruit those with a non-law degree are likely to prove worthwhile in the long term.

Secretaries

Many solicitors fail to make full use of the potential which an able secretary offers to them. There is an unfortunate tendency to regard secretaries as typists, who need even matters of punctuation to be decided for them. It is not unknown for solicitors to dictate their own name in its preferred version on every letter they dictate.

A good secretary, and many in legal firms are excellent, can achieve very much more for her (and sometimes his) legal colleague than a set of accurately typed letters and documents each and every day. It may well be appropriate that the fee earner's diary is managed by the secretary along with the drafting of all routine correspondence that does not require a trained lawyer's attention. By and large employees are better motivated if they are required to work nearer the upper level of their capability rather than the lower and a personal assistant can dramatically improve the output of the lawyer.

A number of colleges provide secretarial training specifically for legal secretaries, with a course that includes legal terminology and general principles of law as well as the core secretarial skills.

Employers of all descriptions have become concerned of late about the falling birthrate and its effect on the job market. The 'demographic trough' is likely to be at its most aggravated in 1995 and there have been various commentaries in the legal press about how law firms may be affected. The general view seems to be that the supply of lawyers will be no greater or lesser a problem than it has been of late, since law remains a popular and competitive degree subject. On the other hand, the ready supply of young secretarial staff which legal firms have traditionally relied upon is bound to be adversely affected. Solutions have to be found to problems and if the demand for legal services remains buoyant firms will have to be prepared to make themselves more attractive to older staff. In practice this will mean adopting a much more flexible approach to part time working and the competing interests of family and children, particularly during school holidays. This in turn might be achieved by replacing the one-to-one relationship that most fee earners have with their secretaries with more of a team approach. Firms might also investigate how much of their keyboard work can be produced on-line from home terminals.

Legal Executives

Considerable efficiency can be achieved by involving legal executives as part of a fee earning team. The American term 'para-legals' is gaining ground in this country and is useful in that it can also include fee earning staff who are not members of the Institute of Legal Executives. It is a mistake to suppose that all legal work requires a full legal training and a professional qualification as a solicitor or a barrister. In many instances unadmitted staff are quite capable of performing demanding legal work better than many of their qualified colleagues and with minimal supervision. The potential to firms of para-legals is twofold. First, they offer a more readily available supply of human resources for legal work of all descriptions; secondly, they provide an opportunity to maintain satisfactory and profitable ratios of partners to fee earners with a greater degree of permanence.

A commitment to training is needed to derive maximum benefit from the use of unadmitted staff. Not only must the firm be prepared to devote a certain amount of the aspiring fee earner's time to training in order to enable him or her to perform at the required level, but in many instances the partners and admitted staff will need management training to learn the necessary delegation skills to make the team truly effective.

Chapter 4
Attracting the Candidates

Advertising for external candidates is the most obvious way of filling any given vacancy, but will not necessarily be the most effective. Advertising can never be a purely scientific activity and is far from being a perfect way of recruiting people into the firm. Apart from the fact that advertising can cost a great deal of money, the administrative burden of dealing with unwanted applications can be considerable. Furthermore, there can be no guarantee that the best candidates will actually see the advertisement placed by the firm.

These factors mean that any practice with recruitment needs should be prepared to adopt a wider strategy for filling any given vacancy. Advertising may well form a part of that strategy, but will not necessarily be the sole or even main device.

It is often helpful to consider the other options first to define the role that advertising should play. These alternatives might include:

existing staff
former staff
recommendations from existing staff and contacts
applicants from previous advertisements
recruitment agencies
selection consultants
search consultants

In this chapter we examine the various options open to firms with recruitment needs and analyse how advertisements can be made as cost effective as possible.

Existing Staff

Most firms tend to close the career options of existing staff once they are part of the firm, with the result that dissatisifed staff tend to move elsewhere to find the new challenges they are seeking. No doubt the partners will not be unduly sorry to see certain members of staff leave the firm, but it must be counted as a failure of the personnel function to see an able employee leave for an avoidable reason. The solution to any such retention problem lies in asking members of staff on the level of satisfaction they feel with their current duties and on presenting realistic opportunities for career growth in conjunction with the firm's training system. It can be excellent for staff morale to encourage training programmes which allow the ambitious to develop and improve within the practice. The cost of failing to do so may be a substantial, but largely hidden, item of recruitment expenditure.

Former Staff

The advantage of attempting to persuade former staff to apply to the firm is that their track record is known within the practice and they are in a better position to decide if they wish to return. At any one time only a small proportion of former staff would probably like to return to the partnership, but many more will be pleased to be remembered, and will quite possibly be able to recommend friends and colleagues who might like to be approached. Contacting former staff is particularly attractive with fee earning staff in narrow specialisms where the field of potential candidates is likely to be limited.

The key to succeeding in the use of such approaches is to consider the reactions of the individuals concerned. Returning to former employers might well be counted as an admission of failure with intervening career moves, so it might be necessary to reassure the former employee that the internal publicity will stress the additional experience gained, or any other positive factors. Former staff represent a highly neglected recruitment source for most firms.

The particular considerations which extend to female staff who have left the firm to start a family and care for infant children were dealt with in Chapter 3.

Recommendations

Former staff are not the only group who are likely to be able to recommend potential applicants: the existing partners and staff will almost certainly be able to make invaluable suggestions if they are asked. To help improve the prospects of success in finding candidates in this way many firms have introduced a bonus scheme in which employees receive a payment for successful introductions. Even if these schemes err on the generous side they are still likely to represent a considerable saving for the partners over agency fees and they also invariably have a positive bearing on staff morale.

Although the potential of recommendations is often overlooked there are certain limitations which should be borne in mind. First, with fee earning staff in particular, the natural competitiveness and ambition of most employees means that they will not necessarily want to recommend friends and former colleagues who will constitute a threat to promotion prospects.

Secondly, the practice of internal recommendations is likely to be discriminatory if the existing ethnic balance within the firm is unsatisfactory. This has occupied the attention of the Commission for Racial Equality in respect of a number of higher profile large scale employers and may well require positive steps in other aspects of recruitment activity to redress any inherent discriminatory bias.

Previous Applicants

The great advantage of this recruitment source is that they can be regarded as being 'free', if the costs of locating them in the first place are assigned to the previous recruitment exercise. All that is required is that the practice is prepared to make the effort to keep details on file, together with a qualitative rating if the applicant was seen at interview. Investigating such records is much less demanding if they are maintained on computer, and quite simple systems are likely to achieve satisfactory results.

Again, former candidates may be flattered to be approached, and may well be able to recommend other potential applicants if they are no longer interested themselves.

Recruitment Agencies

There is a distinction of orientation between agencies and consultancies. The recruitment agent is essentially 'candidate-driven' and conducts business in which candidates are identified and counselled by the business and are then introduced to potential employers. Fees arise on an opportunistic basis: if the firm employs a candidate introduced by the agency it will pay an agreed fee based on the initial starting salary of the employee. Without placements the agency receives no income.

A consultant works more closely with the employer, and will often be retained by the firm to identify and introduce suitable applicants. It may well be that fees are paid in part on a retainer basis for the advice which is provided by the consultant from time to time and this is likely to be supplemented with a percentage fee if and when an appointment is made.

The distinction is more difficult to draw in the specialist field of legal agencies and consultancies, since many agents build up a close working relationship with certain legal firms. Furthermore, many consultants also operate as agents in respect of candidates that make themselves known to the business. Many agencies also take a justifiable pride in the 'consultancy' role they adopt towards individuals who approach them about the desirability of a career move.

All agencies and consultancies have to be registered under the Employment Agencies Act 1973, an Act which also prohibits certain undesirable practices in the sensitive process of dealing with individuals and their careers. Most firms are prepared to accept candidates from any agency since the quality of the applicant is usually seen as the sole issue of significance, assuming that fees are within the normal scale. There are, however, some firms that operate a policy of only dealing with agencies that they have approved individually.

Selection Consultants

The selection consultant works closely with the client to plan its requirements and then supply them. The partnership might benefit from the expertise of the consultant in this area of recruitment, the first task often being to plan the precise requirements of the firm. Once the job analysis is completed, and a job description and person specification have been agreed, the consultant will advise how suitable applicants can be identified.

The benefits of involving consultants in the recruitment process are:

- the firm may not be able to handle the considerable amounts of paperwork which certain plans might entail;
- outside expertise can introduce objectivity to discussions which have been inconclusive or contentious, or where the firm simply cannot risk making a mistake;
- advertisements placed by the consultant can be made anonymous, with the result that confidential plans need not be identified within the firm; salary levels will

not become public knowledge to the embarrassment of the individual later appointed and the firm is free to change its plans without loss of face if it wishes.

Search Consultants

The growing adjunct to selection consultancy services is headhunting, or search consultancy. There are those who are aghast at the prospect of one professional firm seeking to entice away the staff of another through a paid intermediary, but others would argue that there is little moral distinction between placing an advertisement in a journal which the firm is happy to purchase for its staff and telephoning the intended readers direct to see if they have noticed it. In some instances the pool of desired specialists might be so small that it will be sensible to avoid the inevitable wastage of the conventional job advertisement. In practice most firms are likely to take a considerably more jaundiced view of the 'can we talk?' telephone call than whole pages of seductive job advertisements.

Few headhunters are likely to bite the hand that feeds them and will probably decline instructions which will result in approaches to the staff of existing clients. If staff shortages increasingly apply to narrow specialisms headhunting will almost certainly continue to grow in its relative importance as a means of locating suitable candidates.

Advertising

By now the firm should have a clearer idea of whether it does wish to advertise and, if so, whether this should be in conjunction with any of the other methods described above. A photocopy of the advertisement should always be posted on suitable noticeboards and might even be circulated individually to the relevant class of employees. Whatever the other methods of attracting candidates, however, the principal aims must be:

- to enable the firm to produce a shortlist of several suitable applicants; and
- to minimise the volume of unsuitable applications.

There may well be subsidiary objectives in placing the advertisement, general publicity for the firm being the most common, but any such motives must be ignored if they will result in the message being less effective in the primary aims.

It is helpful to regard there as being four main stages to the advertising process:

- profile the desired applicants;
- determine the most cost effective means of communicating with that audience;
- prepare and place the message;
- monitor the results – what is the level of response?

Having determined the nature and the content of the advertisement the next important question is media choice. This is relatively straightforward with admitted staff as there are several well known marketplaces for legal recruitment advertisements, but the tactics for support staff will vary more as they are likely to be targeted at the particular geographical area of the firm only. All publications maintain their own data on readership figures and profiles, and most will be able to offer employers media packs which set out the advantages of using their particular publication. It is advisable for all firms to monitor the responses they receive to advertisements placed in particular journals or newspapers, and all candidates should be asked where they saw the position announced. This is invaluable market information which can prevent the future waste of resources and ensure that the process remains as efficient as possible. The information should not be limited to where the successful candidate learned of the job, but should also record the total responses per insert and the figure of net worthwhile responses.

Timing is another important issue at this planning stage. Advertising is most effective if conducted well in advance of the need for the employee becoming acute. Advertising introduces an inbuilt delay into the selection process in that candidates must be allowed time to respond, even to the one-off advertisement and by the time that interviews can be held it is likely that at least a month will have elapsed. The most promising candidates are usually in work already, so will have to serve out their notice period, with the result that at least three months may have passed between advertisement and commencement date. This means that in the case of urgent vacancies it may well be preferable to approach those recruitment agencies and consultancies that the firm has dealings with for a speedier response.

What to say

There is an art to wording job advertisements, but the rules are fairly simple and are easily mastered. All inserts must convey as much relevant information in as compact a space as possible. All job advertisements should also serve to increase the interest of the desired candidates while discouraging others. Too lengthy an advertisement not only represents wasted expenditure for unnecessary column centimetres, but will also fail to convey the information with maximum impact.

Some fascinating clues on what to include in job advertisements emerged in a survey conducted by Price Waterhouse in 1988. The survey was not confined to legal appointments or even professional appointments, but deals in the main with various levels of management which might be said to correspond with assistant solicitor level to partner level. The age range of participants was from 25–60, with 60% of the participants in the age range of 30–45. The particular value of this research is that most available information comes from publications which carry advertisements or advertising agencies, both of whom concentrate on the quantity rather than the quality of impact, whereas this research focuses exclusively on candidates' reactions to actual advertisements. The main findings were:

- 90% did not believe that they were more likely to read advertisements appearing at the top of a page;
- 63% did not think that they read large advertisements and not small ones;
- 68% felt that sophisticated advertisements could over-glamorise a straightforward job (a further 19% had no opinion);
- 84% did not tend to read those advertisements with a picture or design more frequently than others;
- 60% preferred responding to one-off advertisements rather than composite ones, though 19% again had no opinion on this point.

The general interpretation of these findings must be that simple informative job advertising is preferable. This does not mean that there is no role for the eye-catching and unusual, however, and a firm dissatisfied with its normal response may well consider some variation to the routine. If nothing else imaginative typesetting and the use of complementary 'white space' may serve to attract attention amidst pages of similar advertisements. Many have gone further and would no doubt claim to have succeeded in the more competitive market conditions then prevailing. Most legal readers were taken aback by the full page advertisement placed by Denton Hall in the *Times* in 1986, while the subsequent Taylor Garrett (as it then was) series portraying various exotic animals generated laconic correspondence in one of the legal journals. Such efforts must be regarded as having succeeded if the intent was to establish differentiation in what was then an employer-saturated and rather hostile recruitment market.

What then should appear in the effective recruitment advertisement? Where possible salary should be included, and an overwhelming 91% in the Price Waterhouse survey thought that this was important. This research, convincing as it may be, does not necessarily apply with equal force in the recruitment of admitted staff since there are generally prevailing rates which can be referred to. Any announcement that 'City rates will apply' probably does enough to attract the right calibre of candidate in that both firm and applicants will have a shrewd idea of how much is entailed. The term 'market rate' is more vague and less satisfactory, and should generally be avoided.

If salary is to be included it should normally be at the beginning of the advertisement, together with the job title. A brief review of the job and its role in the departmental structure is useful, as may be a summary of the practice and its client base. The person specification must be realistic, and the minimum experience and other qualifications should be stated to discourage undesired candidates, and emphasise to suitable applicants that the level is commensurate with their expectations. Location will often be apparent, but should be stated if it is not. Finally, directions should be given as to how to apply and some simple reassurance that the application will be treated in confidence is usually advisable.

Some do's and don'ts

Do

- Be realistic about the position on offer and its potential
- Be enthusiastic about the practice and its future
- Indicate the salary or its approximate level
- State location
- Describe in general terms the nature of the firm and its clients
- Refer to the duties to be undertaken and the place they have in the departmental structure
- Set out minimum qualifications required

- Refer to desirable and important personal attributes
- Give details of how to apply
- Be consistent in the use of house style, and use the firm's logo if one exists.

Don'ts

- Ramble on – be concise!
- Scare off good candidates by describing the ideal
- Mislead the readers on the job content
- Show any sexual or racial discrimination

Chapter 5
Selection Interviewing

The personal interview still holds sway as the sole method of personnel selection in most legal firms, notwithstanding recent evidence that interviewing is one of the least reliable means of identifying suitable employees.

The process of choosing staff assumes particular importance in the professional services sector for two reasons.

The quality of service which the firm can offer to its clientele depends directly on the quality of its legal and support personnel. The quality of legal advice is regarded by most lawyers as the most important differentiating factor between them and their rivals, and this has therefore to be regarded as a highly important factor.

The second factor is the direct economic cost of recruitment decisions, especially given the dramatic increases in salaries which the legal profession has witnessed in recent years. A number of firms have undertaken calculations of the cost of training legal staff. One of the most interesting, revealed to the authors by a leading City firm for publication on an anonymous basis is as follows:

	£
Fees and maintenance for the trainee at Law School	
Law graduates	5,000
Non-law graduates	10,000
Attributable charge of recruitment budget overheads	7,500

Estimated cost of time expended on training and supervision of trainee by qualified legal staff	25,000
Salary and National Insurance over two years	37,500
Average and approximate total	75,000
Less fees earned by trainee over two years	25,000
Cost to the firm per trainee	50,000

Note: All figures approximate, especially that relating to fees earned during training, which can be considerably higher in the case of better trainees.

Calculations of this type could easily serve to undermine the confidence of the partners and others charged to select staff for the firm, but partners tend not to be so critical in hindsight of employment selection decisions as equivalent capital expenditure decisions. Nonetheless, it is well worth considering the wisdom of appointing trainee solicitors to start at the firm two years hence on the basis of one short interview only, especially if, as above, the practice also offers generous financial assistance to see the candidate through his or her professional examinations.

In one respect partners are at an advantage in selecting legal staff in that they are examining suitability for a job they have direct and personal experience of, which is not always the case in commerce and industry. Alternatively, this could be seen as a weakness in the general level of recruitment practice in solicitors' firms, in that the participators in the selection process are not compelled to articulate the criteria which they consider to be important.

In this chapter we will examine principles of recruitment interviewing. In Chapter 6 the potential of other selection procedures is investigated, with particular emphasis on psychological testing.

Interviewing

Good interviewing is an art, but following a few basic guidelines can add considerably to the effectiveness of the process. The main steps are:

- preparation
- introduction
- information gathering
- information exchange
- conclusion
- follow-up.

1. Preparation

It need not take long to prepare for an interview, but doing it well, and doing it thoroughly, will pay dividends later. Preparation is particularly important if several individuals are involved in the interview, since it is advisable to reach a consensus in advance as to the format that the session will take.

First, objectives should be clarified. Is this to be a shortlisting exercise, or a final interview? What action will be taken following the interview and when might the candidate expect to hear from the firm? There should be agreement on the requirements and this may require a discussion if no job description exists. Ideally the practice should develop criteria on which decisions can be made to help keep subjective elements in proper proportion; a person specification is invaluable in this respect.

Next the pre-interview data on the candidate should be analysed. The candidate's application form or CV is likely to lay down the basis of the interview discussion. If academic qualifications are important to the firm the interviewers might well ask questions about their attainment. Experience with other firms is likely to be of greater interest than other areas of the applicant's background, but it is important to ask questions about the individual's interests to build up a fuller picture of him or her as a potential member of staff.

The right environment should be set for the candidate. Clear instructions as to the time and place of the interview are essential. Candidates should be expected and greeted, and liaison with the receptionists is important in this respect. It is advisable to deal with the potentially embarrassing question of expenses on arrival and before the formal interview. Many firms overlook the fact that first impressions of the firm are as important to the candidate as first impressions of the candidate are to the interviewers. A courteous and efficient reception is important.

The seating arrangement in the interview room should encourage easy communication. The discussion should be allowed sufficient time to run its course and a safety margin should be built in for exceptional candidates. Hurried interviewing should be avoided at all costs.

2. Introduction

The introductory stage of the interview should be used to break the ice between the two parties and to set the stage for the type of interview to be adopted. This is a good opportunity to introduce the practice and the interviewers. The structure of the interview should be outlined and the candidate should be told what the firm aims to get out of the meeting. All of this should help to put the candidate at ease. As far as possible it is advisable to get rid of interview nerves: doing so successfully will ease communications. Deliberate stress should be avoided at all costs unless the interviewer is qualified to interpret it. Partners who interview aggressively to see if a candidate can cope with pressure usually succeed in promoting the firm as hostile and unfriendly and learn little about the candidate as a potential employee. The aim should be to conduct a probing interview in a relaxed environment.

3. Information gathering

The introduction will be handled exclusively by the interviewer: in the next stage of the process it is the candidate's turn to do the talking. The information gathering stage is the core of the interview. Its purpose is to check information on the candidate and to probe areas of relevance to the post.

Techniques vary and should be adapted in line with the vacancy being discussed. In an unstructured interview the candidate is asked to explain his or her personal history along his or her own lines. This approach has the advantage that the candidate is allowed the freedom to highlight areas of particular interest or concern and further probing by the interviewers into these areas can reveal useful information. At the other end of the spectrum a structured interview will elicit direct responses to particular questions about past experience. This is likely to be more appropriate in respect of lower level vacancies and when dealing with candidates who do not have a career track record, such as undergraduate applicants for articles. In either case the interviewers should retain firm control while allowing the candidate to express him or herself freely.

The interviewer should ask 'open' questions which should create the opportunity for a discussion, rather than 'closed' questions which merely invite a 'yes' or 'no' answer. Contrast, for example, 'Did you enjoy your articles at McGregor & Co.?' with 'How do you look back on your articles at McGregor & Co.?'

Two other dangers are multiple questions, which are long and rambling, and which confuse interviewer and interviewee alike, and the 'leading' question which implies the anticipated response.

Listening skills are also important. Few of us are naturally gifted listeners but the good interviewer will listen and watch for every word and intonation. Good awareness of candidates' reactions to questions may well help to reveal areas of concern which should be investigated further. Positive listening also has the advantage of building a good relationship with the candidate who is more likely to feel that his or her responses have been properly listened to. The effective interviewer must also be prepared to tolerate silence while the candidate considers his or her reply. The sympathetic interviewer may have to combat the temptation to prompt the answer that he or she would like to hear.

It is useful to bring the information gathering stage to a close by a summary. This will reassure the candidate that he or she has communicated important information, and is also a useful way of defining a clear end to this stage of the interview and introducing the next.

4. Information exchange

The interviewer should now have a sound base to move on, and so discuss the details of the job on offer. The candidate should be given details of what the job entails, what role it plays within the practice and such benefits that go with it. The aim at this stage is to ensure that the candidate will have sufficient information on which to base his or her decision to accept an offer of employment. The unsuccessful candidate also needs to be treated well at this stage, not least because every applicant is likely to recount his or her experiences to at least one other lawyer, so the image of the firm as an employer is therefore at stake.

Finally the candidate should be offered the opportunity to raise any outstanding questions. This is the last chance for the applicant to deal with any points that he or she feels have not been dealt with and the choice of questions often reveals a good deal about the candidate and his or her concerns.

5. Conclusion and follow-up

The interview should now be brought to a close. The candidate should be told what will happen next and informed when he or she will hear from the firm. If a medical examination is needed or if references are to be taken up the candidate should be told what will be involved. The candidate should be escorted back to the reception area, and thanked for his or her time in attending the interview.

In most cases the decision to appoint the applicant, or to invite him or her to a further interview, will be made immediately after the interview. It is advisable not to begin by expressing strong statements of opinion, but the panel should individually assess the candidate in terms of the criteria agreed at the outset.

Follow-up procedures should then be observed on the timescale indicated to the candidate.

Interview Checklist

1. Preparation

- Ensure candidate has clear instructions of when and where to attend.
- Make arrangements for the candidate to be expected and greeted at reception.
- Book the room and arrange for suitable refreshments.
- Circulate relevant paperwork to interviewing panel.
- Arrange for possible substitute interviewers if there is a risk that one or other or the panel will not be able to attend.
- Meet the other interviewers before the time set for the interview. Determine:
    the roles to be played by the participants
    aspects of the candidate's background requiring detailed questions
    the decisions which can be made at the meeting.
    what follow-up should be suggested to the candidate.

2. Introduction

- Deal with interview expenses claim before the formal interview commences, before the candidate is brought into the interview room.

- Introduce the firm to the candidate, and explain the nature of the interview.

3. Information gathering

- Ask open questions of the candidate to build up a profile of the record of the candidate and his or her demeanour and interests.
- Listen carefully to all the replies of the candidate and watch for 'non-verbal' signs of stress or discomfort which suggest that the candidate lacks confidence in his or her replies.
- Listen and watch.
- Summarise the information gathered in this stage of the interview.

4. Information exchange

- Provide details on the job, its role in the firm, and any benefits going with it.
- Invite the candidate to ask any questions to deal with uncovered points.

5. Conclusion and follow-up

- Inform candidate of medical and references procedures and when the candidate will hear from the firm.
- Accompany candidate to the reception area.
- Evaluate the candidate individually in terms of pre-determined criteria.
- Observe follow-up procedures on the timescale suggested to the candidate.

Case Study

Mills & Reeve of Norwich and Cambridge is one of the increasing number of firms that combine partners and a personnel manager in selection interviews, particularly for trainee solicitors.

An hour is allowed for each undergraduate interview. Expenses are dealt with by the manager before the interview. We do not interview from behind desks or tables and try to arrange the room so as to put the candidate at ease. A clock is put on the wall behind the candidate to avoid the embarrassment of looking at our watches as the interview progresses. All interviews are attended by the personnel manager and one, or sometimes two, partners. The personnel manager introduces consistency by attending all interviews and opens the interview by introducing the other interviewer(s) and explaining the structure of the session. She then asks questions about the candidate's school record, taking the questions up to the time the interviewee went to University or Polytechnic. The partner present then takes over to ask about degree studies and the interest in becoming a lawyer and usually a question designed to elicit the candidate's analytical skills. Once these questions have run their course we deal with any questions the candidate wishes to raise and we then ask one of the present trainee solicitors to show the applicant around the offices. We encourage applicants to ask whatever they like of the person showing them around and we do not check what was said after the event. An informal lunch is also held at the end of the morning in order for candidates to meet each other and some of the partners and staff. The lunch does not form part of the selection process.

Charlotte Points and Mark Jeffries: Mills & Reeve

Chapter 6
Psychological Testing

Interviewing is something that we all believe that we can do well. Most of us like to think that we are a shrewd judge of character, and that a brief interview will be sufficient for us to assess the potential of a candidate as an employee of the practice.

Unfortunately, our perception of our abilities often runs ahead of reality. Faced with evidence of the unreliability of interviewing as a selection tool, and the significance to the well-being of the firm of the decision to appoint staff, a number of firms have examined the potential of other selection methods to complement selection interviews. Prime amongst these is psychological testing, which is perceived as offering the advantage of introducing scientific objectivity into the selection process. Unfortunately, many such firms seem to have experimented, only to revert to traditional interviewing alone soon afterwards. Where there has been dissatisfaction it seems to be on grounds of cost and uncertainty as to usefulness.

In this chapter we examine what is involved in psychological testing, and explore the limitations to it. What difficulties might be encountered, and are they worth overcoming?

Testing's Potential

A psychological test can be defined as a set of tasks upon whose responses inferences may be made regarding the attributes of the individual. One of the most rapidly expanding facets of the recruitment scene in recent years has been the use of such tests. This rise in popularity has brought about an increase in the number and variety of tests available, accompanied by competing claims from their proponents as to their suitability for employers' requirements. Nonetheless, the overall usage of tests in recruitment selection remains low and there is little evidence of their use being as widespread within the legal profession as it is elsewhere.

Behind the increasing interest lies a good deal of hard evidence that testing can be a highly effective tool for assessing ability and potential performance. Furthermore, much of the evidence casts severe doubts on the reliability of recruitment interviews as a method of making satisfactory recruitment decisions. In a recent Institute of Manpower Studies report over 96% of those surveyed felt that interviews were 'very reliable' or 'quite reliable' as predictors of future performance, but only 11% were prepared to describe interviewing as an objective or unbiased method. However, the same report goes on to claim that interviews are the least reliable method of assessing the suitability of an individual for a job, as tested against the supervisor's view of the performance of the individual after appointment, promotion prospects, success in training, and the length of time they spend with the organisation (Employee selection in the UK).

What can be tested

Psychological tests can be divided into two broad categories:

> Ability tests: which show how well or how poorly an objective test is performed; tests within the ability family include aptitude, which measures the potential capacity to acquire a skill or proficiency, and achievement tests which assess objective levels of skill and knowledge.

> Personality tests: in which the individual is asked to provide insights into his or her personal make-up.

Ability tests measure such aspects as verbal reasoning and

numeracy, whereas personality tests, which are almost invariably conducted by questionnaire, reveal information relating to personal qualities and motivational factors. Where legal firms have been attracted to testing at all it is usually in the field of personality rather than ability. The firm seeking articled clerks will accept the grade of degree and often the institution which awarded it, as all the evidence it requires of intellectual ability and training potential; when seeking new secretaries it is likely that attention will focus on secretarial examination successes, and so on. The particular circumstances of the legal firm mean that educational achievements are normally required to enter the pool of potential applicants for any given position. It is within the sphere of personality, the grey area where there are no examination certificates to point to, that the real key to future potential probably lies. It is the lack of objective data on personal attributes which makes testing an attractive adjunct to the essentially subjective process of the selection interview.

Personality Testing

There can be little argument that personality is one of the prime ingredients in determining whether an individual is likely to succeed within a given position. Definitions of personality dwell on the distinctive personal characteristics that we possess that influence the assessment of us by others. Many practices seek to assess personality on the basis of the interview alone, but the interviewer's own views and perceptions will often mean that systematic analysis of the candidate is impossible. Research has shown that numerous extraneous factors affect the evaluation of candidates, including the order of seeing candidates and various personal attributes or interests of the candidates which trigger reactions in the interviewing panel. These subjective reactions often manifest themselves in the 'halo effect', in which a favourable response becomes likely to a candidate, or the contrasting 'horns effect', in which the candidate is blighted by some unfortunate aspect of his or her background or demeanour.

The first attempts to evaluate personality traits concentrated on physical characteristics. Although we might now scorn ancient categorisations such as the four bodily humours which were said to correspond to the four fundamentals of the Universe, there are many today who form personality prejudices on the basis of physical appearances.

Simulation exercises are widely used in the Armed forces to investigate leadership, communication skills and sensitivity. Although such exercises are high in 'candidate appeal' by being clearly relevant to the employer's legitimate selection criteria they have their limitations, such as in testing anxiety or emotional stability.

The use of personality questionnaires is on the increase, no doubt in part because of the inadequacies of other methods of reaching conclusions on relevant personality traits. Most personality questionnaires are normative, in which the individual is required to express preferences between two or more types of behaviour. This contrasts with ipsative tests in which the replies to questions are either right or wrong. The relevance of this distinction is that the former tests merely produce a scale of preferences appropriate to the individual, and not 'scores' which can be compared to other candidates.

The first personality questionnaire to be developed as an aid to selection was Woodworth's Personal Data Sheet, which was used by the US Army in the First World War. Numerous tests have since been devised, but it is important to stress that personality testing is still not a precise science and perhaps is incapable of ever being so. The whole question of personality is an area of social science and so is subject to the imponderables and variables that physical sciences alone can exclude. There is little agreement amongst specialists in this field as to how many personality factors can be measured in a reliable manner, although it is encouraging to note that one of the most ambitious – Cattell's 16 personality factor model – is one of the most generally accepted questionnaire tests. The 16 PF test was developed in the United States after the Second World War, and received a British standardisation in 1972 by Dr Peter Saville. It is a test recommended for use in the legal profession by Bob Scott of Middle Management Resources who explains its relevance as follows:

> The 16PF test is the most widely used and best validated questionnaire. The test measures 16 key personality dimensions which can be used to predict future performance. Behaviour, personality and style (all of which are examined by the test) are such critical influences in the success of professional advisers that their evaluation must be a prime consideration in selection and placement decisions.
>
> Psychometric testing provides information about candidates which would not otherwise be available. Used in conjunction with a properly conducted interview it might add between 5–10% to the total recruitment costs, but will provide about 50% of the information on which the final decision should be based.

There is one fundamental weakness of personality testing which should be stressed, which is that it is a mistake to regard any individual's personality as being a fixed set of drives, desires and inhibitions which he or she will be endowed with for life. Personality is an ever-evolving package of responses which changes with age and experience. This might be particularly relevant in the selection of articled clerks where, in the normal course of events, two highly formative years will elapse before the successful candidates commence their training with the firm.

Choosing Tests

In deciding whether the practice should use tests there should first be an assessment of how well current techniques are working. If there is room for improvement, tests should be considered and consultants should be contacted. The planning and administration of psychological tests is not a matter for amateurs and the British Psychological Society controls their use fairly tightly. The consultants will attend to the strict regulations surrounding the administration of the tests and analysis of the results. The names of authorised consultants can be obtained from the Society or from the Institute of Personnel Management, which has produced a Code on Occupational Testing which should be consulted by any firm wishing to implement tests.

There are a number of important points to check with any consultants that the firm makes contact with. First and foremost the practice should verify that any test is free of inherent bias on grounds of race or sex; there is a good deal of debate at present into the potential of tests to discriminate against certain groups. In addition, trial data should always be made available on any test to explain its theoretical structure, and show how it has performed in practice. Although such data can appear somewhat daunting there are several main indicators that a prospective user should investigate:

Validity. Does the test actually measure what it is supposed to? The consultant might refer to 'concurrent' validity which measures stated qualities against some pre-existing assessment, and 'predictive' validity which assesses future potential. A correlation score of 0 denotes no relationship with pre-existing data, while a perfect score would be 1. In practice good tests vary between 0.2 and 0.5.

Reliability. Can the test achieve similar results from similar groups or individuals under the same conditions? Reliability clearly has a major bearing on validity. Correlation scores should be high: generally in excess of 0.65.

Effectiveness. Has the test been used satisfactorily in similar circumstances before? Ideally it should be possible to contact other legal firms, although it has to be accepted that the number of consultants with experience of solicitors is still limited.

Established Norms. Some indication should be given with normative tests of how specified groups perform on them. Unfortunately, published evidence of the patterns in successful lawyers in this country does not seem to exist, but research on accountants for the 16PF test reveals them to be less extrovert and outgoing than managers, more critical and more aloof. They are slightly more sober and serious than the population at large, but are more radical and experimenting. (Saville and Holdsworth Ltd., 1983)

The partners will also need to consider how acceptable the test is likely to be to candidates. There is a paradox here in that we tend to be fascinated in uncovering our own personal traits, yet resist attempts by others to do so in a scientific way. Horoscopes are compelling reading even for the sceptics, but testing seems to smack of 'big brother' in our midst. The key to overcoming candidate resistance is often in explaining the relevance of the chosen tests to individuals, and then in offering to share the findings with them. Candidate resistance may well stem from resentment of what others know about us that we do not. It is also important to consider whether the tests will seem relevant to the candidates. It is one thing for the Royal Air Force to ask applicants to test their co-ordination skills on a flight simulator, but it is quite another for trainee solicitors to be expected to complete numeracy tests which read like one of the IQ papers on the 11 plus examination. The use of tests, in other words, has to be sold to candidates. If the partnership manages to do this, it may well find that testing is something which has 'candidate appeal' and which may help to profile it as an enlightened and professional employer.

Factors for and against

The Institute of Manpower Studies research paper referred to above revealed that only 16% of participating companies used occupational tests, but it also uncovered widespread ignorance and misunderstanding on the potential of testing in the recruitment process. In the 16% that did use tests they were found to be considerably more reliable and valid than conventional recruitment methods alone, so it seems fair to conclude that the use of tests is likely to increase if occupational psychologists can continue to present the evidence to their commercial clients and price their services reasonably.

Unfortunately, tests are time consuming and, because skilled assessment must be made of results, they are not cheap. Candidate resistance can be a problem, although sensitivity to the feelings of candidates may convert the use of tests to a positive advantage.

Of the other methods of testing the potential or personality of an individual only graphology is worthy of mention. There are firms who have used graphology with satisfaction, especially on senior appointments. The extent to which any practice should rely on this form of testing should be determined by their own quality of experience if they do decide to experiment with it, in the absence of conclusive evidence either way of its efficacy.

Summary

The importance of making correct recruitment decisions will be readily apparent to most in private practice. What each firm must do is to decide if current procedures are working satisfactorily, or if improved interviewing technique is all that is required. If it would be desirable to inject objectivity into what must essentially be subjective assessments of personality the weight of available evidence is that testing is likely to prove the most effective option. The special importance of the choice of trainee solicitors, coupled to the lack of career history of most applicants, may well mean that firms should give particular consideration to employing such tests on undergraduate applicants for articles.

Chapter 7
Offer and Acceptance

By this stage of the recruitment process the firm will have interviewed the short-listed candidates and will also have selected those it wishes to appoint. There may well have been some discussion with the candidate about likely starting dates at the interview or subsequently by telephone and it may seem as if it is now merely a matter of awaiting the arrival of the new employee. Attention will still have to be paid, however, to the correspondence which confirms the appointment, and certain other formalities might also have to be attended to. In this chapter we examine all the factors which arise in converting the job offer into a binding contract of employment.

In some respects it is possible to regard this phase of the recruitment process as having two distinct main purposes. First, and most obviously, the practice will be seeking to deal with the legal formalities of the contract being finalised, but it is also possible to regard medical examinations and job references as forming the last stage of the selection process. It is easy to overlook the invaluable information which can be gleaned on candidates at this stage and it may well be advisable to aim to obtain as much information as possible on potential offerees before confirming the offer of employment.

Four separate subjects arise in this area, the first two of which can claim to be part of the selection phase. The other topics are concerned with agreeing formal terms and smoothing the eventual induction process.

- References
- Medical examinations

- Legal formalities
- Maintaining contact

References

There is a view that references are hardly worth the paper they are written on. There are those firms that disregard them altogether, while others go through a curious ritual of collecting a considerable amount of largely worthless information. Both such practices are unfortunate. The reference is the last chance to avoid what could be a very costly mistake, but will only operate as such if the firm is prepared to structure the reference request as a deliberate attempt to gather useful information and if it is then prepared to examine that information with care.

A distinction should be drawn between personal referees and previous employers. It is difficult to regard the personal reference as being anything other than a superficial testament to honesty and decency on the part of the potential employee. There may be little harm in asking such referees if the candidate has convictions for dishonesty or other such troublesome features, but only the most direct of questions are likely to elicit any damaging information, since even the most obtuse of candidates is likely to nominate referees who will volunteer a positive view. The one exception to this general rule is with academic references where a greater degree of objectivity can usually be relied on. The lack or absence of an employment history with younger recruits increases the desirability of obtaining references of this kind.

Where an employment history does exist the reference of a previous employer can be very much more helpful than personal reference from friends or acquaintances. As a matter of general policy the candidate's permission should always be obtained before any reference is taken up. No doubt the responsible firm will liaise carefully with the candidate in respect of the timing of taking up references, but it is worth bearing in mind that although the IPM code allows references to be taken up from previous employers at any time, an approach to the current employer is only permitted once an offer has been made. This will mean that a firm should consider making all offers of employment subject to the obtaining of satisfactory references and the letter of offer should make it clear that positive references are a condition precedent of an offer of employment.

The partnership might ask the following of the current employer, or of any of its predecessors:

- the dates of employment (checking the months as well as the years will reveal if there are any gaps which the CV glossed over)
- the job title and details, which in the case of admitted staff may mean confirmation of departmental membership and relevant experience
- as discreetly as possible, information on the individual's
   timekeeping
   attendance
   commitment
   integrity

The more sensitive the question, the more direct and specific the question needs to be. On attendance, for example, it is better to ask:

'How many days did X miss through illness in his last 12 months with you?'

rather than:

'Was X's attendance satisfactory?'

Sometimes the current employer might be highly sensitive about losing the employee in question, in which case information may be provided grudgingly, but if circumstances permit there are two highly illuminating questions to ask:

'If X were to be applying to you again would you be prepared to employ him again?'

and

'Do you know of any valid reason why X should not be employed by us?'

Interpreting the reference also requires skill and judgement. The recipient needs to be as alert to what has not been said as to what has been said and particular attention should be given to what appear to be guarded and qualified compliments. A firm employing a new cashier, for example, should see danger signals in any reference not referring to the honesty and integrity of the individual concerned. Where any such doubt arises, contact should be made with the referee to request further and better particulars, perhaps in writing, but more probably by telephone.

The aim of the staff partner or the personnel manager in taking up references should be to gather as much relevant information as possible, but it would be unfortunate to characterise the referee's position as being to withhold damaging information unless specifically requested to disclose it. The legal and ethical position on giving references is not exactly black and white, although the main principles are well established. The law of defamation applies to references, but the defence of qualified privilege applies since the information is given in pursuance of a duty to a recipient who will have a corresponding interest in receiving it. In *Riddick* v *Thames Board Mills* (1977) publication to a secretary who typed the allegedly defamatory statement was held not to break the ambit of qualified privilege. As common lawyers will testify, defamation has several well publicised deficiencies which make legal proceedings unlikely, but solicitors of whatever ilk will contend that avoidable risks are generally best avoided. Since the truth of any statement is a defence to any claim in libel or slander, allegations which could be defamatory should only be communicated if proof of their veracity exists.

This cautious approach is further advisable if the legal position of the confidentiality of references is examined. In theory references are given in confidence, and should not therefore come to the attention of the individuals they refer to. In practice, confidentiality cannot be guaranteed, and there have been cases of alleged unfair discrimination in which references have formed part of the employer's case, and so have been disclosed within proceedings. In the vast majority of cases the employer can be confident that the reference will be received in confidence and respected as such, but because of the risks which do exist in the case of adverse references it is understandable that relevant information is only given if it is specifically requested.

The special requirement of integrity and honesty in the provision of legal services gives particular pertinence to the Rehabilitation of Offenders Act 1974. Under the Act there is a general duty on the part of employers not to disclose spent convictions. Furthermore, an individual who can show that a spent conviction was referred to on grounds of malice can claim damages for defamation, thus giving rise to the unlikely situation of a plaintiff succeeding in a claim for libel or slander notwithstanding the truth of the offending statement. Since lawyers are exempted from the main statutory protection of not having to refer to spent convictions when applying for employment it will be fair to question referees about such information in respect of admitted staff. With support staff greater care is needed in order to ensure that no claim of malice can reasonably be substantiated.

In conclusion, references should be regarded as an important aspect of the pre-appointment procedures and the prudent firm will be willing to embark on what might amount to an interview of the current or previous employer if there are grounds to suspect that the recommendation is tainted in any way. It is advisable to make it clear to candidates that all offers of employment are subject to the obtaining of satisfactory references and care should be taken not to overlook the invaluable information on the individual which can be obtained at this stage.

Medical Examination

There is no statutory obligation on employers to conduct pre- or post-employment medical examinations on their staff, other than in the case of specific groups of employees who are covered by particular pieces of legislation relating to certain occupations. Although legal offices can therefore claim to be exempt from any specific duty to examine the health of the potential employee the general obligation of the employer under the Health and Safety at Work Act 1974 to ensure, so far as is reasonably practicable, the health, safety and welfare of all employees at work is relevant and a pre-appointment medical examination can be useful in a number of regards:

- to assess the fitness of individuals to do the job for which they are employed;
- to obtain information on any special medical needs which require particular attention during the course of employment (such as might arise in the case of conditions such as diabetes or epilepsy);
- to obtain data on the individual so that any subsequent deterioration in physical well-being can be monitored.

In practice a medical examination is more likely to be necessary if the firm operates its own occupational pension scheme, in which case a successful medical examination will probably be required as a condition of entry to it.

If the practice does wish to commission a medical examination there are two broad avenues open to it:

- Invite the prospective employee to see his or her GP for a medical examination. This will entail asking the appointee for details of his or her doctor and writing to them to request a brief report, referring to what the job entails and any particular aspect of health that the firm would like to be checked.
- Alternatively, the firm can contact a local GP and arrange for him or her to conduct all medical examin-

ations on its behalf. This makes the administration of conducting examinations simpler, but the procedure might become awkward if the new employee lives in a different part of the country. A combination of both systems is probably therefore advisable.

Whichever system is adopted the detailed records will remain with the GP: the firm will receive a summary in return for the fee.

Legal Formalities

There are few firms which cannot lay claim to at least one employment law specialist who can be called upon to advise the partnership on its documentation and procedures, but a brief summary of the position might be helpful.

There is no requirement that the contract of employment must be in writing, but the Employment Protection (Consolidation) Act 1978 does require employers to give the employee a written statement of terms not later than 13 weeks after the beginning of an employee's period of employment. The details which must be covered are contained in section 1 of the Act and, briefly, include:

- the identity of the parties
- the date of commencement of the contract of employment
- whether any previous employment with a prior employer counts as part of the employee's continuous period of employment and, if so, the date that it began
- the scale or rate of remuneration
- the intervals at which it is paid
- terms and conditions relating to hours of work
- holiday entitlement
- sickness provisions
- pension schemes and arrangements

Offer and Acceptance 63

- the length of notice by either side to terminate the contract
- the job title.

Section 1(4) of the Act requires that the rules relating to disciplinary and grievances procedures are also set out. The most common practice nowadays is to confine the offer letter to a quick summary of the key points within the employment contract and to leave the bulk of the employment relationship to be dealt with in the written statement of terms and conditions. This is less the case with unusual positions such as senior support staff or partner designates where the letter of offer will amount to the basis of a more individually negotiated contract, but even then it is advantageous to refer to annexed documents such as the job description as far as possible. The letter of offer might therefore usually be confined to:

- job title
- commencement date
- permanence of employment
- salary or rate of pay
- provisions relating to overtime
- office hours
- car scheme
- separate allowances (call out on night work etc)
- commitments above normal hours and duties.

If the offer of employment is conditional upon a medical examination or obtaining references this should also be clearly stated.

The paperwork can be further simplified by employees being referred to documentation which is available, but which is not sent individually to every new employee. This is permitted by section 2(3) of the Act with the proviso that the employee must have reasonable opportunities for reading it in the course of his or her employment, or that it is in some other way 'reasonably accessible', such as an office manual.

Two final points are worthy of mention in this respect. First, it is advisable to introduce as much flexibility as possible into the original terms in order to avoid problems later on. If the development of national firms gathers pace legal firms may soon have to observe the advice they have often given to industrial clients to define the location of work as broadly as possible in order to be able to require certain members of staff to relocate to another office. Secondly, and in similar vein, it is helpful to specify how individuals will be informed of subsequent changes to their initial terms and conditions.

Maintaining Contact

With all the formalities attended to and the offer of employment now accepted, attention can turn to induction. Although this is the subject of the next chapter it is well worth the firm considering induction as starting before the formal commencement date. In any sphere of activity, first impressions are important and a further letter nearer the commencement date confirming how much the partners are looking forward to the new employee starting at the firm is likely to pay dividends, particularly if it comes from the departmental head or leader. If the appointee has indicated that he or she is going on a holiday before starting at the firm the letter should say how that the writer hopes that it will be enjoyable.

Efforts in this direction are particularly important in the case of trainee solicitors, who are often recruited a full two years before they join the firm. Life at the firm may continue much the same during this time, but the trainees may start to feel that they have little to do with the firm as the months, years and examinations pass by. Students appreciate attention continuing to be paid to them after they are appointed: birthday, Christmas and examination congratulations cards can do a great deal of good in convincing the new recruit that he or she has made a sound decision in accepting the offer of articles made by the firm.

Finally, it is worth noting a worrying trend to have developed during 1990 – the act of some firms in unilaterally cancelling offers of articles previously made in good faith. The reasons for doing so have often been regrettable, but obvious, with the downturn in work experienced by many firms causing a major reconsideration about staffing levels. Revoking offers of articles once they have been accepted is clearly an extreme measure which no firm should take lightly, and the disruption to the careers of the offerees is quite evident. Not surprisingly it is a situation which has occupied the attention of the Trainee Solicitors Group, who comment as follows:

> The Trainee Solicitors Group is alarmed by offers of articles being withdrawn, in some cases only months before the student is about to commence employment. Whilst the Group sympathises to an extent with the firm we can only deduce that the situation reflects bad planning, which of course is not helped by the trend of offering articles in some cases over two years in advance of commencement.
>
> What is alarming is the manner in which some of the cases which have been brought to the Group's attention have been handled. In some cases where financial assistance has been provided through the Finals course there is no indication as to whether the student should repay the money, causing further embarrassment and stress. The situation is a difficult one, but the Group feels that some sensitivity by firms faced with the decision would make a great deal of difference.
> (Fiona O'Kane: Past Chairman, TSG)

Interestingly, the Group does not recommend litigation in these unfortunate circumstances and refers members instead to relevant agencies. Some cases have also been referred to ACAS with some success. This disturbing new trend gives further poignancy to the contractual consequences of recruitment decisions by firms.

Chapter 8
Induction

Induction is the process of helping new employees to settle into their positions in the firm as quickly as possible. For the first few weeks or months continual appraisal is needed to iron out problems as they arise and before they become aggravated; furthermore, the firm must take positive steps to identify the further training needed by the employee in order that he or she can adapt to his or her new role. All of this is in addition to the orientation to the practice and its offices conducted by most firms, along with the customary introduction to relevant colleagues.

Time and money expended by the firm in attracting and recruiting promising candidates may well have been wasted if it then fails to give appropriate attention to induction procedures. If disillusionment sets in at this early stage the starter may well subsequently fail to realise his or her full potential with the practice. On the other hand an effective induction procedure will provide a solid base for future performance and development.

The point has already been made that induction should not be regarded as starting as late as the new employee's first day. There is an argument that induction starts at the earliest stage of the recruitment process, when the candidate first applies to the firm. The potential employee will begin to make value judgements on the firm and its culture from his or her first dealings with it, so it is important that all dealings with candidates throughout selection procedures are efficient and courteous. Pre-commencement induction must certainly extend to ensuring that the new employee is left in no doubt as to when to first appear at the firm and should also embrace maintaining contact with the recruit if a considerable period of time will elapse between appointment and commencement.

Induction is sometimes seen as little more than a rather altruistic gesture on the part of the firm to ease the transition of the employee into the ways of the practice. Good manners certainly play a part in the induction process in seeking to put the nervous and rather vulnerable new employee at ease within the firm, but effective induction also makes good business sense. The sooner the new employee can relax into his or her new position, the sooner he or she will be able to make an effective contribution to the work of the firm.

In summary, there are three reasons for developing and maintaining good induction procedures:

- improving the prospects of retaining promising staff;
- showing a considerate attitude to new employees at a time when they will most appreciate it;
- enabling the new recruit to be as effective as possible at an early stage.

Contents of Induction Programmes

Induction is essentially a two way process in which the firm must make efforts to discuss the experiences of the new employee. In addition, the provision of information by the firm to its new staff will be a crucial aspect of any induction programme and this information might be classified as follows:

- the position
- the environment
- the people

The Position. The tendency not to produce job descriptions for professional and secretarial staff is a potential difficulty in inducting new staff in these areas. The purpose of a job description is to ensure that all parties have a clear and agreed understanding of what the position entails. Not only does this serve to remove much of the doubt that the employee may feel about the level of responsibility attached to the position, but it will also constitute objective criteria for evaluating the progress of the employee during the probationary period and beyond. Where no job description exists proper attention must be given to ensuring that the employee is fully briefed on the tasks and responsibilities that the partners will look to him or her to assume. In those situations where there is a job description time should be set aside to discuss its contents in such detail as is necessary to ensure that all misunderstandings are eradicated. In all cases the new employee should be left in no doubt as to the standard expected of them and the objectives they will be expected to achieve; the traditional attitude that 'you'll pick it up as you go along' should be regarded as unsatisfactory. This approach – often termed 'sink or swim' – puts the retention of promising staff at risk. Once they are settled into a firm most people tend to forget how alien everything appeared at first, whatever their career or academic record before joining the firm. Early misunderstandings can cloud not only the partners' assessment of the individual, but also the individual's assessment of the firm.

The Environment. The larger the practice, the more likely it is that a first day tour of the entire offices will not be helpful: it might even do more harm than good. It is certainly desirable that the employee should come to terms with the office layout as soon as possible and office maps can be very useful in this respect. On the other hand, it is unrealistic to expect anyone to remember a complex maze of offices or the names and faces of more than a handful of people at any time, especially when they are ill at ease and somewhat tense in their new environment. If the purpose of the tour is therefore also to introduce individuals from the firm, consideration should be given to staggering this into a number of different tours throughout the first week with the firm. The organisers of any induction process must be careful not to present new staff with a bewildering visit to all parts of the office that leaves them confused as to their whereabouts, nor so many random introductions that they fail to remember those people that they have met.

The People. It is preferable to concentrate on ensuring that new staff are introduced to those people that they are likely to have direct working relationships with. This will extend beyond immediate secretarial and fee earning colleagues and supervisors into the realms of the support staff, such as the accounts department. Where introductions are made they should be backed up with a written list of names and if the firm is able to maintain head and shoulders photographs of the partners and relevant staff and make printed copies available, this will be of considerable assistance.

Timescale

It is unreasonable to consider that all the objectives of an induction programme can be met within the space of one working day. Formal induction should be regarded as extending over the entire probationary period, in which case it will have five general phases:

Greeting and introduction

It is essential that the new employee is expected on his or her first day and is properly welcomed. At this stage the starter mut also be given basic information on the firm, an intelligible explanation of the office lay-out, information on relevant employment policies and other matters of general significance. In most cases it should be possible to cover most or all of this during the first day at the firm.

Job orientation

Next it is necessary to move away from the general and work on the specific challenges which face each individual within the firm. Usually following straight after the general introduction, and taking at least part of the remainder of the first week, this is the start of integration into the department or specialist group and will include a detailed review of job contents and a personal introduction to relevant colleagues. It is vital that, if at all possible, a desk or other place is prepared for the new employee by the time that they arrive at the firm.

Training needs

An assessment of the new skills or know-how which will be required by the new employee in order to succeed in the tasks ahead should be conducted, and agreement should be reached on how these matters should be dealt with.

Continuing liaison

For the first few weeks there should be continual liaison between the employee and his or her supervisor to ensure that both parties deal with problems as they arise.

Termination of probationary period

At the expiry of the probationary period there should be formal confirmation that the employee is now a permanent member of staff, and there should also be a constructive discussion on the employee's future development with the practice.

The Psychological Challenge

It is helpful to delve into industrial psychology to gain a deeper insight into the induction process and its importance. The concept of the 'culture' of the firm is a useful starting point.

Induction

All organisations can be said to develop their own individual cultures. One helpful definition is:

Culture is the commonly held and relatively stable beliefs, attitudes and values that exist within the organisation.

Although attempts to categorise just what the culture of any given firm might be are almost certainly doomed to failure, it can be observed that every firm has something about it which differentiates it from others, and which can be said to amount to its own special 'culture'. In appraisal reviews one of the most frustrating conclusions, for both sides, is that the employee does not seem to fit in. More often than not this can be taken to mean that the employee has not succeeded in adjusting to the culture of that particular firm. There may be various explanations for such a failure: perhaps the individual feels that there would be too much of a compromise of his or her essential values to conform, or perhaps he or she is not sufficiently sensitive to perceive what is required of them to do so.

Induction should succeed in giving numerous clues to the behaviour and attitudes which prevail within the practice, but can never provide a comprehensive blueprint for success. It would be unfortunate if the firm were to be so narrow-minded that only clones could expect to succeed and it is hoped that individuals joining the firm will be judged on objective criteria as to their worth to the practice rather than personal prejudices. Nonetheless, there are those who are judged a failure because they fail to attune to the firm's culture. In such situations the partners may well pronounce that the individual in question is 'not one of us', or alternatively might seize upon some shortcoming in the employee's work performance and place undue emphasis on it to blight future development within the firm.

Early in the induction process the new employee will, probably subconsciously, be trying to assess what is required of him or her to adapt to the culture of the firm. The partners and existing staff can help in this process and should try to remember how alien the firm must have once seemed to them. Trainee solicitors might experience particular difficulties in attempting to adjust from student values to those prevailing in their chosen sphere of private practice. Frequent discussions between the new member of staff and the supervisors should assist in the essentially personal process of adjusting to what will be regarded as acceptable behaviour.

It might also be helpful to observe that cultures will not be fixed and are likely to be constantly evolving with the changing composition of the firm and any changes in its professional activities. Any one individual is unlikely to be able to make any significant alteration to the firm's culture over a short period of time, but with patience and persistence he or she might be a contributor to change.

The second area of industrial psychology which it is helpful to consider in respect of induction is the area of work motivation. There are numerous theories which seek to define the reasons which lead us to use such endeavours as we do at work, the more recent of which are considerably more complex than the satisfaction theory first espoused by Aristotle. There is evidence to suggest that employees are more highly motivated if they understand the overall goals and aims of the organisation and also understand how their individual role will contribute to it. It is therefore important that the partners explain future plans for the firm and the department in order that new members can feel that they share these aims and objectives.

Finally, the induction supervisors might pay some attention to the manner in which groups operate. If a new employee is taken around the firm there will be those who are quick to smile and introduce themselves, while others are more naturally wary. This difference is not only a matter of individual personality, but also reflects deeply rooted attitudes to group membership. Problems have arisen in industry and elsewhere with initiation rituals which pose physical danger to those who aspire to join the group. Even in the more polite office atmosphere of the typical solicitors' firm the new employee will find efforts to gain acceptance into the group an important contribution that they have to make to the induction process. Those who fail in this regard are, unfortunately, unlikely to be retained by the firm for any considerable period of time.

Mentoring

The traditional induction procedures of most employers have only two parties – supervisor and employee. The starter is also likely to seek advice and assistance from those about him or her, but on very much of an ad hoc and informal basis. This system may not be as helpful to the employee as one would like: the individual might feel awkward about continually seeking directions from the partner or manager in charge, and might also feel it unfair to pester busy colleagues with questions that are likely to seem rather trivial to them. Mentoring is a process gaining favour in commerce and industry which may help in this respect.

Mentoring consists of designating an individual to be available to advise and counsel the new employee. The mentor is not directly involved with the supervision of the employee's work, and could either be superior to the individual in the hierarchy of the firm, or could be someone of equivalent age and status. It should be possible to identify potential mentors within the firm and training of anyone being considered for the role should always be regarded as a necessity. In certain schemes in industry the mentor is required to provide formal reports on the 'protegé', but it seems fair to contend that schemes are more likely to succeed if they are understood to be a recognition of an essentially informal and confidential relationship and not part of the control procedures of the practice. The mentor can be a guide and friend to the employee and can also deal with the more personal aspects of being part of the practice and adjusting to its culture which would not always be appropriate for manager and employee to discuss.

There is a further value in mentoring schemes in private practice, in that associates or senior solicitors may well be the most appropriate mentors in most firms. If so, they are provided with an opportunity to experience an aspect of personnel management and to prove their worth as managers if they hope to become partners with the firm.

The Training Input

Induction has been put onto a considerably more professional footing in many firms in recent years, largely because of the significant improvements which have been made in training. In those practices that employ their own training directors or managers, trainee solicitor induction is often regarded as an important aspect of their duties, largely because trainee staff require a greater volume of technical information to be conveyed to them in order to begin to contribute to the work of the firm. Public courses are available for those other firms that do not have their own training staff. The induction of admitted staff, on the other hand, is usually a matter for the particular fee earning section, or the personnel department, or both. The firm is in a better position to organise trainee solicitor induction programmes since those involved join as a group at the same time or times during the year, whereas other staff join at any time. It is important that the individual training needs of new employees are not overlooked in induction discussions and attention will need to be given to the formal training that is required to enable the new employee to perform his or her role to the required standard.

Case Study

The City firm of Freshfields is one of the largest employers of trainee solicitors in the country and has developed an induction system which is designed to take trainees through their period of articles and beyond. Unlike some of its competitors it does not operate an intensive full time programme lasting for a week or more at the outset, preferring instead to commence the programme with a two day introductory course, followed by a progressive series of law and skills seminars.

The two day introductory session provides a bird's eye view of where we are in our marketplace and envisage the firm developing in the future. We deal with internal matters such as how management decisions are made and how the departments work together. Much of the emphasis is on getting to know each other as a group and also the important contacts they will need to know in the firm. We recognise that it would be unrealistic to expect the new staff to absorb all these details there and then, so a 'starter's pack' of written information is also supplied. This also provides details for the new trainees on where to find the information they will need.

The other major aspect of this initial induction programme is to explain what it is that trainees do within the firm and we deal with some of the basic skills in such areas as telephone technique which are needed from the outset. Likewise there are practical sessions on the use of the library and our information bank.

This initial programme is followed up by shorter departmental introductions in the area of each trainee's first seat. Subsequently, and at intervals throughout their training period, we provide practical skills sessions, and introductory, or 'newcomer' seminars explaining the basics of a transaction or other aspects of work. All induction training is made as practical as possible in order to be directly relevant to the duties that the trainee is actually undertaking within the firm.

(Sally Woodward: Director of Education and Training)

Summary

Induction should be regarded as a vital part of the recruitment process and is the first stage of a retention strategy for any practice. Induction commences before the employee joins the firm and should include a formal introduction to the main procedures and policies of the practice. Each individual employee should be given a full review of what is expected of them and should also have the significance of their contribution to the growth of the practice explained to them. Induction extends to the end of the probationary period, and should embrace frequent discussions about the performance of the individual throughout his or her first few weeks with the firm. Observing these procedures should maximise the possibility of the appointment proving successful, with the employee not only adjusting to the firm relatively easily, but also going on to develop a rewarding career with it.

Chapter 9
Employment Records

All employers need to collect and maintain certain information on their staff. Although some of this data is required to be kept by law, most employee information merely serves to assist the partners in the efficient administration of the practice. The manner in which these details are stored will be dictated by the size of the firm in question and by any particular requirements that it might have.

This chapter consists of a brief summary of the records that any firm might expect to maintain. We also deal with issues to arise from the need to keep sensitive and confidential details in-house, including the relevance of the Data Protection Act 1984.

Areas requiring Records

1. Personal details

Full details are needed on the individuals within the firm, covering such basic information as name, age, sex, educational record and next of kin, as well as national insurance number and tax code.

2. Pre-employment paperwork

Information collected before the employee joined the firm should be filed as it will continue to be relevant for a number of administrative purposes. This information will include:

Application form (if any) and letter of application
Curriculum Vitae
Interview record
Test results when relevant
References
Medical reports.

It might be advisable for the partners to agree a policy on how long different aspects of this information should be stored. References in particular might not need to be retained substantially beyond the expiry of the probationary period. A medical summary will continue to be useful in the event of accidents or illnesses at work, though for ethical reasons the full medical record will remain outside the firm under control of a medical practitioner.

3. Terms and conditions

The Employment Protection (Consolidation) Act 1978 contains the requirement that all employees must be provided with a written copy of their terms and conditions within thirteen weeks of commencing at the firm. Although the Act does not provide that this statement must be stored, it is clearly necessary that a copy is kept on the relevant file in order that any disputes as to the initial agreement can be resolved. In similar vein, the original offer of employment and all subsequent changes to the original documentation should be filed carefully.

4. Employment history

Remuneration record
Benefits paid
Career progression
Appraisal records
Attendance records
Copies of any disciplinary action
Training history

Accident details, if any.

ACAS provisions make firm recommendations that certain disciplinary decisions should be recorded in writing and maintained for future reference.

Particular attention should be given to the maintenance of training records in respect of professional staff. The compulsory continuing training regime is soon likely to be extended and will then apply to the majority of partners as well as their staff. No partnership will wish to take the risk of failing to obtain practising certificates for solicitors within the firm. Training records should therefore not only provide evidence of what activity has occurred, but should also provide early warning of any training shortfalls.

5. Salary information

Full details on salary, tax, national insurance, pension contributions and statutory sick pay must be maintained in order that they can be open for Inland Revenue inspection. Employers now bear a much greater responsibility for the administration of Statutory Sick Pay, and rules of the Departments of Health and Social Security require records in this area to be maintained in such a way that inspectors can have access to them on request.

6. Accident details

Details of all accidents at work are important in the administration of various benefits and also serve to assist the partners in ensuring that risks are avoided where possible. The main piece of legislation in this area is the Reporting of Injuries, Diseases and Dangerous Occurrences Regulations 1985. These rules require the firm to notify the enforcing authority by the quickest practicable means of death or certain serious injuries sustained at work. In addition, all incidents causing injuries which result in absences of three days or more must be reported. A standard HSE form is available for the purpose. All organisations should also maintain an accidents book, and the entry of details of any incident should be regarded as an important discipline

7. Management information

In addition to the above records in respect of the individuals within the practice, information should also be compiled on broader personnel issues in order to assist the partners in the management of the firm. There is no point in collecting information merely for the sake of it and effort should only be expended in creating records if they will be consulted and used. Firms might benefit in particular from analyses of employees by age, sex and time with the firm. Even the most informally managed firms will also want to know its total salaries bill and other relevant statistics might include absence details and patterns, and staff turnover.

8. Equal opportunities

Compiling records that show racial or ethnic origin is not free from controversy, through fear of how such information can be used. Nonetheless, the Commission for Racial Equality stresses the role that such records can play in the promotion of equal opportunities, as does the Equal Opportunities Commission.

Form of Records

Many firms find a manual system completely satisfactory for their purposes, perhaps with the addition of salary payments being organised through the accounts computer. The larger the practice, the more likely it is that computers will be needed to cope with the volume of data and actions required.

Whatever the form that employee records take, the importance of confidentiality should be recognised. Compiling and maintaining personal information does create the responsibility for ensuring that the information is used for its proper purposes only and that it is available only to those with a legitimate interest in its contents.

There are two principal advantages in maintaining employee records on computer systems:

- speed and accuracy of data retrieval;
- efficiency in storing large volumes of data.

On the other hand, many partnerships tend to overlook the time that is required to load up relevant information and the use of computers requires not only further investment in terminals and other hardware, but also training for all personnel staff.

A firm which currently operates a manual system should consider carefully whether the investment of time and money in switching to a computerised system will be justified. Much will depend on the size of the practice, but the complexity of information which the partners are likely to require is a further important consideration. Many of the personnel management software programmes which are generally available are designed to cope with much greater complexity of user enquiries than most firms tend to demand. A typical small or medium practice is unlikely to want to conduct surveys of mean educational achievements of the staff, absence patterns throughout the year, or other similar exercises and is therefore likely to find a well maintained manual system completely satisfactory for its purposes.

It is often helpful to divide the records into three categories:

1. Personal file

Relevant pre-employment documentation (CV, medical summary, correspondence etc);
Next of kin and details of where they can be contacted;
Career summary details, with records of appraisals;

Disciplinary notes and copies of letters and warnings;
Training records

2. Holiday and absence records

Full files might not be appropriate; record cards kept in an accessible index system might be preferable.

3. Salary and financial information

This might often need to be stored within the accounts department in order that salary administration can proceed smoothly.

A partnership considering the computerisation of its records should develop its criteria before examining the options available, with the most important factors probably including:

- user friendliness
- speed and ease of access
- flexibility; can it cross refer data or be extended?
- compatibility to the main accounts and salaries system
- systems support after installation.

Data Protection Act 1984

The Data Protection Act has not proved to be the major regulatory problem that many anticipated at the time that it first became law. The demand for advice on the Act by commercial clients has been less than expected, and enforcements and prosecutions have been comparatively rare. Nonetheless, personnel records do fall within the potential ambit of the Act and must therefore receive the attention of the partnership.

The Act was designed to 'regulate the use of automatically processed information relating to individuals and the provision of services in respect of such information'. Personal data is any information about an individual, but excluding any indication of the intentions of the data user in respect of that individual. Within the current context firms are data users, while the employee would be termed the data subject. The Act only applies, however, if use is made of computerised systems, since they alone involve the use of 'automatically processed information'. Manual systems are outside the scope of the legislation.

In research conducted by Derek Torrington and Laura Hall before the publication of their book *Personnel Management – a new Approach*, the greatest concern expressed by personnel managers in respect of the Data Protection Act was the seventh of the data protection principles.

> An individual is entitled to be informed where data is held about him and is entitled to access to the data and where appropriate to have the data corrected or erased.

The implications of this principle should be considered carefully by a practice considering the computerisation of its records. The Act gives individuals the right to see any expression of opinion about themselves, but not indications of the intentions of the data users in respect of the data subjects. More relevant to legal firms is the obligation to register the personal data they hold and their purposes in so doing. Furthermore, data users must adhere to the various principles set out in the Act, which include rules that personal data shall:

- only be held for specified, lawful purposes;
- be adequate and relevant to the purposes they relate to;
- be accurate and kept up to date;
- have appropriate security surrounding them.

The Act also creates rights of subject access in order that data subjects can enforce their rights in respect of inaccurate information.

The formality of registration under the Data Protection

Act and the need to observe the terms of the Act may be a further advantage in firms retaining manual systems if they appear to meet the needs of the partnership. Alternatively, the partners might consider adopting a greater degree of openness in respect of its records and announce that it will operate an 'open file' system in which all employees can have access to their own file. Those organisations which have adopted this approach have often found them to be beneficial in reducing the atmospher of secretiveness which can irritate members of staff and in helping to keep all records correct and up to date.

Confidentiality

Finally, it is important to stress again the need to ensure that adequate safeguards exist to protect the confidentiality of employee records. The importance of confidentiality is referred to in relevant IPM and ACAS codes and is also a principle contained in the Data Protection Act. Personnel staff and accounts staff handling salary administration, must possess qualities of discretion and the partners must stress the importance that they attach to confidentiality when appointing any such staff. The partners must deal with any breaches of confidentiality that come to their attention promptly and firmly.

Chapter 10
Appraisal

Appraisal schemes are becoming very much more commonplace in private practice. The idea is growing that partners should make the effort to inform members of staff how they feel that they are progressing and that there should be a deliberate attempt to discuss the individual's achievements and shortcomings. The performance appraisal may well be linked to the salary review, particularly with more senior fee earning staff where strict salary bands tend not to apply.

Despite the obvious attraction of adopting a procedure which seeks to get the best out of the firm's personnel, contradictions tend to emerge when discussing appraisal schemes. First, although there is general agreement within the personnel profession on how to conduct recruitment interviews and draft job descriptions, there is no standard appraisal scheme which is claimed to possess general application. There is instead widespread acceptance that appraisal schemes must be in line with the style, culture and objectives of the organisation in question, with the result that schemes tend to differ according to the particular environment in which they operate.

Secondly, despite the near universal agreement that a well-structured appraisal system will benefit the organisation, personnel professionals find great difficulty in reporting schemes which meet with general acclaim and approval. Appraisal, for all its potential, is not a popular process. Participants on both sides often regard the process as being unduly bureaucratic. Furthermore, there is a genuine difficulty in criticising people we work with and rely on, or in being criticised if we are being appraised. A degree of bureaucracy will usually be necessary to persuade managers to conduct honest assessments of their staff.

Appraisal schemes tend to be time-consuming for all involved. This has to be regarded as a particular problem given the pressures of private practice. The implementation of any scheme might be time-consuming, but with care and commitment an appropriate appraisal scheme ought to provide long term benefits to the firm by enhancing the retention and development of its human resources. Appraisals, in common with other areas of personnel management in private practice, are an investment in future efficiency.

Objectives

There are a number of different forms of appraisal, the objectives of which differ:

Performance reviews

These are the standard career appraisals relating to the activities of members of staff, and have as their aims the improvement of individuals' performance within the practice.

Reward reviews

Salary reviews are often held in conjunction with performance reviews, and in any event the connection between the performance appraisal and rewards should be explained.

Potential reviews

These serve to review the longer term issues of the individual's career prospects within the firm, and will involve an analysis of past record, current performance and personal attributes to assess the potential of the individual.

Clearly all three forms of appraisal tend to overlap in practice, but there are advantages in separating them where possible. The performance appraisal can provide objective data for the deliberations of the salary committee, but it should not dictate what the rate of increase, if any, should be. Important details such as the link between the performance appraisal and salary reviews must be clearly explained to appraisers and appraisees alike. It is also important that all concerned should approach appraisals as a constructive opportunity to assist personal development and enhance motivation. Difficulties ought not to be avoided, but criticism should be offered in a constructive manner in order to encourage improvement, rather than condemn.

The performance appraisal is the major form of review, and the one which tends to be of the greatest interest to partnerships. The two fundamental objectives of performance appraisals should be to provide the employee with a development step, and bring about an increase in the individual's motivation. More specifically the appraisal meeting should:

- review the past performance of the individual;
- agree on future performance objectives;
- identify developmental needs, perhaps in areas such as management or inter-personal skills training;
- allow criticism of the firm and its procedures if the individual feels that they have hindered his or her performance.

It is important to stress that a marked difference exists between appraisal meetings and disciplinary procedures. The poor performer who is failing to meet the required standard of performance should expect to have this explored at appraisal. A primary objective will then be to develop and agree an action plan to assist the individual to improve. If, after subsequent review, and for no valid reason, the necessary improvement has not occurred formal disciplinary action might become appropriate to rectify the situation (see Chapter 11). It is important that appraisals are understood throughout the firm to be essentially positive in nature, where difficulties will be aired and discussed openly in an attempt to improve performance. Drawing the distinction between appraisals and disciplinary meetings should go some way to lessening the tension which often seems to accompany appraisal interviews.

Developing an Appraisal Scheme

The published work in this area stresses the need for any appraisal scheme to operate within the particular culture of the organisation in question. Furthermore, since the firm's culture is likely to be evolving at any given time it follows that appraisal schemes should themselves be subject to continual assessment. This latter point was one of the most noteworthy features to emerge from an extensive research exercise into appraisal schemes conducted by the IPM in 1985; one-third of all schemes surveyed were then less than three years old.

In planning an appraisal scheme the partners must also be prepared to deal with the reluctance that many of the appraisers are likely to feel in respect of appraising staff with whom they work closely. This potential difficulty is overcome by:

- providing all appraisers with effective training into the interpersonal skills required to conduct constructive appraisal meetings, and ensuring that all such individuals understand and are committed to the aims of the new appraisal system;
- designing a paperwork system which requires value judgements to be made by partners and other relevant managers during the course of the appraisal interview.

The first objective is to determine the key data which needs to be drawn from the appraisal meeting. The paperwork will then be designed with this in mind, including supporting notes and directions. There are numerous variations on an essentially common theme, but the main contents must be the rating by the supervisor of the individual's performance in a number of regards such as:

- technical competence;
- problem solving abilities;
- motivation and enthusiasm;
- interpersonal skills within the office;
- client care skills;
- overall assessment.

Qualitative ratings are usually invited, most commonly on a number scale of 1–5, or perhaps up to 6 or 7. The supervisor should be allowed the option to decline to express an opinion on a particular area on grounds that he or she has not observed this trait sufficiently to be able to comment fairly. The form might also allow the appraiser to express an opinion in narrative form, perhaps to explain the background to a performance mark. There should also be an accompanying set of directions to explain how the form should be completed.

The form to be completed by the appraisee will usually require comment on his or her:

- main achievements;
- difficulties experienced;
- areas for improvement;
- training needs;
- career development objectives.

It is important that partner commitment is manifested in the delivery of the programme. Realistic deadlines should be set for all stages of the process, as delay in conducting appraisals can be a source of tension on the part of the employee and can serve to undermine motivation. With this in mind the system should be as user-friendly as possible. All firms should insist that documentation is completed and returned within the agreed time limits and if the personnel manager or assistant experiences difficulty in persuading one or more of the partners to observe these standards, the procedure must be enforced from within the management structure of the practice.

The Interview

The interview is fundamental to the appraisal system. The difficulties of holding the interview should be recognised, and appropriate training should be given to all who will be required to conduct these important meetings. As with all meetings, preparation is important and those conducting the interview must ensure that they have assimilated the major points to emerge from the information available to them.

Consideration should also be given to the environment, which should be informal so as to encourage all involved to relax.

Many of the skills of conducting an appraisal interview are exactly the same as for selection interviews, and a similar structure should be followed. The appraisal interview can be said to fall into four distinct phases:

- the introduction, where the manager gives a clear explanation of the objectives of the meeting and the nature of it; particular attention should be given to eliminating nerves if possible;
- the exchange of views, in which the assessments of all concerned are discussed;
- the purposive stage, in which the appraiser uses one of the strategies set out below to agree a course of action constituting a development step and motivation growth;
- the closing stage, which is where agreement is summarised, or differences are crystallised; a clear plan of action for self development and all training needs should be recorded.

The main strategies in appraisal interviews tend to be:

1. 'Tell and sell'

The manager is likely to have decided upon a strategy prior to the meeting. The aim is therefore to adopt a 'selling' role where he or she must persuade the individual of the line decided and secure the individual's agreement to the assessment and prognosis. It is important if adopting this approach to ensure that the employee feels involved in the process, as by listening carefully to the subject's version of affairs, before 'selling' the proposed plan of action. Failure to do this is likely to cause defensiveness which will impede implementation: it is important that the individual feels as if he or she has contributed to the outcome of the process.

2. Tell and listen

This approach is similar to 'tell and sell', but the interviewer will ask the employee for his or her views after the 'telling' stage. As the manager will already have disclosed his or her views, however, this might cause confusion or resentment on the part of the subject, in which case it may be advisable to adjourn the 'listening' part of the meeting in order for the employee to marshall his or her thoughts.

3. Joint problem-solving

In this style of interview the parties should agree on their common interest in dealing with any problems that have been identified before the meeting. The manager may well start by encouraging the subject on points which are good, but the emphasis will then turn to a discussion in which both sides discuss any weak areas and how they can be dealt with. This approach requires a non-directive style of interviewing in which an attempt is made to portray the two as colleagues working on mutual objectives. This may therefore be particularly appropriate for senior professional staff and in partner appraisals.

Whatever the strategy adopted, the interview process should be resolved with an agreement on what is needed to improve the contribution of the appraisal subject. A form should be prepared and signed by both parties, which records the agreement between them. There may also be a separate and confidential form which records the assessment of the appraisers on the longer term potential of the individual if the appraisal system is understood to form a 'potential' review also. If the performance appraisal has a bearing on the next salary review, decisions will have to be made on the level of increase, if any, within the timescale agreed.

Pitfalls and Dangers

Properly planned and conducted appraisal schemes will have a major bearing on the efficiency and motivation of the lawyers and other staff within the firm, but badly conducted interviews also have the potential to do more harm than good. Legal employers have a particular problem in being very slow to forget any error made by an individual within the firm. Because the need not to make mistakes is so important in legal work, there is often a tendency to regard the career of a solicitor as being permanently blighted if they have ever made an error of note in client work. Recruitment agents will often find reluctant candidates on their books who are there purely and simply because career progression is barred at their present firm by an error made in the past, notwithstanding the fact that there has been no repetition of the problem since. An effective appraisal scheme will require the interviewers to deal with criticisms arising in the appraisal period only and should therefore help in overcoming this problem.

The fundamental reason for using appraisal schemes is that we tend not to like to admit to our deficiencies, but unless we are assisted in dealing with them our performance is less likely to improve. It is important that criticism is

Appraisal

intended by appraisers to be purely constructive, and is communicated in this way. John Hamilton, who has advised a wide range of firms on appraisal systems, stresses the limited amount of criticism we can accept at any one time and recommends that no more than three specific instances are raised at any one time, backed up in each case by hard evidence.

It is also important that partners accept the need not to regard appraisal as a one-off annual or half-yearly event; encouragement and criticism can be very much more helpful if it is given at the time. It is not simply a matter of good manners to thank an individual for a job well done, but it is effective personnel practice also and can be a significant motivator. Likewise, a problem raised and discussed at the time that it occurs is more likely to be dealt with effectively. The appraisal scheme will prove most useful if it serves to summarise a general view which the individual already has an outline impression of, in order that the emphasis can be on future development, rather than past shortcomings.

Summary

Appraisal schemes work to the benefit of the partners and staff alike in producing agreement on how individual strengths can be further developed and difficulties overcome. Rewards, potential and performance can all be the subject of appraisal schemes, although they often merge in practice. It is important that any appraisal scheme is positive in nature and it should be clearly distinguished from disciplinary proceduress.

Any scheme must be in line with the style and culture of the firm itself and performance appraisal should concentrate on assessing the individual's performance against these objectives. Observing the timescale and pre-determined procedures for appraisals should be regarded as an important discipline and appraisers should be trained in how to implement their own firm's procedures.

Chapter 11
Employment Problems

It may seem pessimistic to devote the final chapter of this book to employment problems, but this view possibly represents a strange attitude to the reality of private practice. Problems are a fact of life, not only in our personal affairs, but also in the substantial part of our daily activity which is taken up by work. Few people can genuinely claim never to have experienced problems of one kind or another at work. How these problems are handled and choosing the steps that should be taken, can have a major bearing on the efficiency of the practice and on the motivation of the individuals within it. Dealing with problems in a positive and purposive manner can do a great deal of good for the firm. This is not to say, of course, that problems should be actively encouraged, but it does suggest that resolving difficulties as they arise is an important management function within any partnership.

Warnings and dismissals clearly require attention to the latest developments in employment law. We have chosen not to set out the principles relating to wrongful and unfair dismissals since most firms will have a specialist in this area who can advise on any case that may arise. There are also numerous texts on employment law which the partners are likely to have access to.

Rules and Procedures

The greatest danger in handling disciplinary matters is inconsistency. This is a particular risk in private practice since a number of different partners are likely to become involved with various incidents at different times. Inconsistency can also result from a misunderstanding of what is expected and also in what is regarded by the partners as important. For all of these reasons firms of all sizes should adopt clear rules dealing with all potential problems and ensure that these rules are brought to the attention of all members of staff. The procedure by which these rules will be enforced should also be set out in writing and explained to all concerned.

Unlike appraisals this is an area where a clear line of advice does exist for all employers. Acting under the auspices of the Employment Protection Act 1975, ACAS drew up a code entitled 'Disciplinary Practice and Procedures in Employment' in 1977. In recent years this code has come under close review and an ACAS booklet, 'Discipline at Work', provides guidance on the interpretation of the code. The newer booklet has received widespread acceptance in personnel circles, notwithstanding the fact that technically it does not have the statutory authority of the formal Code of Practice. The booklet is recommended further reading for those with responsibility for establishing rules and procedures within their firms.

Rules should be in writing, and should ideally be contained in the office manual of the firm. If no office manual exists alternative steps should be taken to bring the provisions to the attention of every member of staff. The partners will need to be realistic as to whether members of staff will assimilate standards which are set out in written documents and the more important aspects of the rules should be highlighted and discussed at induction meetings. Particular attention should be given to those staff who have not worked at all before and who might therefore be expected to have much less understanding of what is required of them in an office environment. New members of staff who have not worked in legal offices before should have the professional duty of confidentiality explained to them, as breaches of this duty will no doubt be considered by the partners to be a serious disciplinary matter. Although such matters may seem obvious, disputes become simpler if the facts have been made clear to all concerned.

Rules should cover the following areas:

- absence and the procedures for obtaining permission where relevant;
- timekeeping and procedures for dealing with lateness;
- health and safety, including rules on no-smoking areas, alcohol in the offices and special dangers relating to office machinery and equipment;
- professional standards, dealing with confidentiality, standards of dress at the office and attitudes to clients;
- use of the firm's resources, personal telephone calls in particular, use of the photocopier and theft of equipment;
- gross misconduct, with details of all items that might amount to an instantly dismissable offence.

It is advisable for the reasons for the rules to be explained where possible, as this should serve to lessen any resentment at what might be seen as an autocratic attitude by the partners. For example, the importance of an appropriate standard of dress is better stressed by pointing out that clients will evaluate the service they receive in part on the impressions they form of the offices and the people they deal with in it. Compliance then becomes more likely, and a potential employee problem will have been prevented. Similarly, it can be highly effective to call the staff together, perhaps in departmental meetings, to explain why new rules have been circulated. Most firms suffer from an excess of office memoranda, and resentment can accompany in impersonal memorandum which goes out to all staff stating new rules on use of the telephone for personal calls. Better by far to summon the staff to explain why these rules are needed and to assure the majority that there is no complaint against them individually.

The advice in the ACAS code on procedures is specific and helpful. The major aspects of it are that procedures should:

- be clear, be stated in writing and provide for matters to be dealt with quickly;
- specify whom they apply to, who can administer them and provide for the individual to be accompanied by a fellow employee of their choice;
- provide for individuals to be informed of the complaint against them, for dismissal for the first offence to be limited to cases of gross misconduct and ensure that no penalty is imposed until the matter has been thoroughly investigated; and
- ensure that individuals have the reasons for any penalty clearly explained to them and provide for the right of appeal with a specified procedure.

The later booklet also stresses the importance of procedures being non-discriminatory and applying to all employees if at all possible. The normal stages of the disciplinary process are likely to be as follows:

Counselling

It might not always be necessary to invoke formal procedures and minor offences will often best be dealt with by a quiet word at the right time and in the right place. Counselling is a discussion of the difficulties that have arisen, requiring firmness, but also consideration from the partner or manager involved.

Stage 1 – Formal verbal warning

If counselling fails to resolve the problem a discussion should be held which might result in a formal verbal warning being given to the employee. A careful note should be made of the meeting and kept on that individual's confidential personnel record file.

Stage 2 – Formal written warning

If the formal verbal warning fails to bring about the required improvement, or if the alleged offence is too serious to be dealt with by a verbal warning, much the same procedure should be followed with a view to giving the individual a formal written warning. The letter should be specific as to the improvements that are required and leave the recipient in no doubt as to the consequences of failing to deal with the problem.

Stage 3 – Final written warning

If there is still no improvement notwithstanding the warning in stage 2, or if the offence is very serious, but not gross, a meeting should be held with a view to providing the individual with a final written warning. The seriousness of this penalty should be stated in explicit terms.

Stage 4 – Dismissal

In a situation where stage 3 has not succeeded in producing the necessary improvement, or in cases of gross misconduct, a dismissal meeting should be held. The partners might sometimes consider a suspension if they feel that the situation is capable of being retrieved, notwithstanding the serious nature of the disciplinary offence.

Disciplinary Interviews

Potentially there will be a considerable amount of tension in a disciplinary meeting. Training of all partners and managers who will be involved in such procedures and careful preparation for the meeting will usually help in making the interviews more effective than they might otherwise be.

The overall approach to any such meeting should be to:

- be positive, and encourage improvement where possible;
- be firm, make the necessary points with conviction;
- be prompt, the meeting will be ineffective unless it is held as soon as possible;
- be calm, adjourn a meeting which gets out of control and treat abuse by the employee as a further offence;
- be consistent, check precedents before deciding the penalty.

Preparation is all-important and attempts should be made to investigate the matter fully beforehand. This will help to avoid the frustration of having to adjourn the matter while further enquiries are made. It may also be advisable to inform the individual in writing of what is alleged against them and ask for a summary of their point of view before the meeting. The individual should be told that they can be represented by a colleague if they wish. As with all the interviews described in this book the matter should be regarded as being important and a room should be arranged where there will be no interruptions of any kind. All relevant facts and records should be available at the meeting and it may be advisable to have a second interviewer to take notes. The aim is to establish the truth, so as then to be able to determine the appropriate penalty.

There will usually be six main phases to a disciplinary interview:

1. Introduction

The persons present should be introduced to the individual and their reasons for being there should be explained. Explanation should also be given as to the penalties under consideration and the procedure that the meeting will follow.

2. Statement of complaint

The complaint against the individual should be clearly explained and the evidence put to them. Unless given in confidence written statements from others should be shown to the employee, or they should be clearly summarised.

3. Employee's reply

The employee should now be given the opportunity to explain his or her side of the case. A deliberate attempt must be made to listen carefully to this other version of events, even if it will then be rejected, unless it is clearly deceitful. It might be necessary to question the employee as to their personal circumstances which might have a bearing on the problem which has arisen.

4. Discussion

Both sides having stated their case there should then be a general discussion designed to reach agreement on what did happen and what should be done to put it right if possible. Arguments must be avoided if possible, although clearly this will be difficult in some instances.

5. Summing up

The discussion stage is brought to a close by the interviewer summing up the discussion that has occurred. This should ensure that nothing of significance has been overlooked, and will also form the basis for the note of the meeting which will need to be recorded for future reference.

6. Decision

If appropriate a decision might be made there and then, but the more serious the penalty under consideration the more likely it is that the meeting should be adjourned for an appropriate penalty to be considered further. Before reaching the decision the partners should consider all the factors of the case, including the past record of the individual concerned. If there is still dispute as to what did happen the appropriate test to apply is the balance of probabilities, and not beyond reasonable doubt.

Full time employees with two years service have the right to request a written statement for the reasons for dismissal where the decision is to terminate the contract of employment (s.15 Employment Act 1989). Employers receiving such a request should respond to it within 14 days, unless for some reason it is not reasonably practicable to do so. Warnings should not be left on the employee's file indefinitely and the firm should state in its policy as to when warnings will expire.

Grievances

It is easy to regard employee problems as being essentially one-way traffic, with the partners always being the ones to initiate action under the rules. It is, however, also important that employees should have the right to raise issues that concern them. The rules should make provision for grievances to be dealt with in a co-operative and helpful manner. It is preferable for all concerned that such difficulties are dealt with as quickly as possible, rather than being left to fester and cause resentment. To encourage problems to be dealt with in this way staff must be reassured that raising a grievance will not count against them in any career assessment.

The rules should recognise that the problem may often be a departmental one, so although in the normal case the employee should be encouraged to raise the issue with the head of department, there should also be provision for the matter to be raised with managers outside the department. Clearly tact and discretion are needed to make any such procedure work, and the partners must also be reassured that there will be no disloyalty to them behind their backs. Although such situations are bound to be difficult for those involved, problems must be resolved if the firm is to be able to offer the level of service needed to succeed in an increasingly competitive professional environment.

The procedure in grievance meetings will be different to the disciplinary meeting, in that the onus will be on the employee to explain why he or she has requested the interview. The partner or manager involved must first listen, then discuss and then try to agree a satisfactory course of action to eliminate the problem. It is clearly important that any such action is taken as soon as possible and that all reasonable attempts are made to deal with the problem to the satisfaction of the complainant.

Appeals

Disciplinary decisions can have far-reaching consequences for the individuals concerned and it is therefore important that there should be an appeals procedure for those who feel aggrieved by the decision made in their case. An appeals procedure should always appear in the disciplinary rules and procedures of the practice and should ideally be drawn to the attention of anyone involved dealt with at a hearing.

It is important that the procedure is swift and that all delays are kept to a minimum. The employee awaiting the outcome of an appeal is hardly likely to be as well motivated as the partners would wish and will probably share an interest with the partners in having the matter dealt with as soon as possible. Ideally the appeal should be heard by a more senior individual than person who conducted the first hearing – perhaps the senior partner. In smaller firms where this is not practicable different partners should be asked to decide the matter, but in the smallest of firms where there are simply not enough partners to constitute a different forum the same partner(s) could sit again, but with a fresh mind to the complaints that were before them previously. In such situations the appeal is likely to be more of a review, particularly if new evidence has come to light.

In the appeal hearing the employee bears a greater responsibility to contribute to the session, so after a brief introduction to the meeting, its purpose and its powers, the interviewer should ask the employee to state his or her case. This should then be summarised by the interviewer, probed if necessary and then a decision should be made, preferably after an adjournment.

The practice is in a difficult situation in hearing appeals. There may be conflicting interests in upholding the authority of the partner or manager who heard the dispute in the first instance and reaching the appropriate decision. If it is apparent that the earlier decision was wrong or misguided fairness must be imposed, even if it causes irritation in the partnership. Tact will help, and it might be advisable to ask the earlier parties to re-consider in order to save face. Those involved must be prepared to take unpopular decisions, however, or the system of appeals will be devalued, and the partnership the poorer.

Summary

Disciplinary rules and procedures are in the interests of partners and staff alike. If the firm lays down clear guidelines on what is expected many problems might be avoided altogether, but where such situations do arise the partnership will be in a better position to deal with problems, and prevent their repetition. Employees must be encouraged to air their grievances without fear of repurcussions to their career. All disciplinary problems should be dealt with firmly, but also with tact and in the hope of solving difficulties where possible. Disciplinary and grievance procedures should enable the partners to be more consistent in the decisions which do need to be made; in the long term fairness and consistency are priceless commodities in the internal management of the practice.

Appendix A

Recruitment Consultancies and Agencies specialising in legal staff

WHY USE CHAMBERS & PARTNERS?

With all the agencies around, why use us?

Because we're professional in our approach: our senior consultants are themselves professionally qualified lawyers.

We know what we're doing: founded in 1973, we are Britain's longest-established independent recruitment consultancy specialising in the legal profession.

We're the right size: with eight consultants in London and Manchester, we provide a fast and efficient service, while still giving clients our close personal attention.

Our Services:

Advertising: the full service is offered, from copywriting to choice of media, vetting responses, interviewing, and submitting the shortlist. (No extra charge for this service.)

Register Search: we have thousands of lawyers on our register, and can quickly search for those matching your requirements.

Executive Search: we have many years' experience in 'headhunting' lawyers, especially for senior positions in industry.

Contacts:

Private Practice: Michael Chambers. *Industry:* Sonya Rayner.

CHAMBERS & PARTNERS
74 Long Lane, London EC1A 9ET
Tel: (071) 606 9371 Fax: (071) 600 1793

BADENOCH & CLARK

Professional Legal Recruitment Specialists

At Badenoch & Clark, we are committed to providing a professional service — which means understanding your business and your needs. This means reacting quickly to recruitment problems and always working to provide the best possible answers.

We also understand our own role. We are a service organisation and we never forget this:

Our Business Exists to Serve Your Business.

With an established reputation in the legal recruitment world, we have an extensive network of contacts throughout the UK, in private practice, commerce and industry. No client is too large and no firm too small to benefit from our service.

Our specialisations include:-

- Construction
- Banking & Finance
- Matrimonial/Family
- Insurance
- Insolvency
- Commercial and Civil Litigation
- Intellectual Property
- Shipping
- Corporate Finance
- Company/Commercial
- Property
- Private Client
- Corporate Tax

Our candidates are Solicitors, Barristers, Legal Executives and Legal Cashiers, at varying levels of experience, from junior clerks to Senior Assistants. We have additional experience of supplying partners and specialist teams where appropriate. We will advise and support you throughout the recruitment process, providing additional information on market trends and salary structures. Our consultants are always happy to arrange meetings to discuss your needs, and work to maintain the highly personalised approach for which we are renowned.

For further information on any of our services please contact Mandy Browne, Manager of the Legal Division in our London office and she will advise on your best course of action.

16-18 New Bridge Street, London EC4V 6AU.
Tel (071) 583 0073. Fax (071) 353 3908.

Aqua House, 24 Old Steine, Brighton BN1 1EL.
Tel (0273) 571490. Fax (0273) 571495.

Neville House, 14 Waterloo Street, Birmingham B2 5TX.
Tel (021) 631 4211. Fax (021) 643 7305.

BADENOCH & CLARK
recruitment specialists

Lipson Lloyd-Jones is firmly established at the forefront of legal recruitment in London and nationwide.

We are dedicated to providing a proficient, professional and comprehensive service to candidates and clients alike.

Our team of consultants are all qualified lawyers with practical experience gained within private practice or industry and in some cases, both. Our City location, together with our unique inside knowledge of the legal profession guarantees that we constantly receive approaches from the highest quality lawyers seeking career advice and advancement. We have an affiliate US company.

Lipson Lloyd-Jones also provides a dedicated advertising service for clients with specific requirements both in private practice and industry, offering advice on copy, design and the most appropriate medium in which to advertise.

Our philosophy is simple; we provide prompt, professional and informed advice of the highest integrity to candidates and clients alike.

For further information contact: Simon Lipson

**Lipson Lloyd-Jones Limited
127 Cheapside
London EC2V 6BT**

Tel: 071-600 1690   **Fax:** 071-600 1972

Michael Page Legal
International Recruitment Consultants

Michael Page Legal was founded in 1984, initially recruiting solely for private practice, but rapidly developing a leading position in the industrial and commercial sectors.

Michael Page Legal now enjoys a leading position in legal recruitment throughout the UK. As well as catering for the London legal community, there are offices in Bristol, Birmingham and Leeds, comprehensively covering the rest of the company.

In addition to outstanding recruitment services, the consultants are expertly qualified to offer career guidance to lawyers at all levels of qualification and in every variety of practice.

By virtue of their experience, both in the profession and specifically in recruitment, consultants understand clients' particular recruitment needs and are able to offer detailed and practical advice on such matters as, for instance, salary rates.

Michael Page Legal consistently registers solicitors with the appropriate qualifications and experience required by every category of firm and is therefore able to meet the widely differing needs of practices and companies throughout the profession.

Michael Page Legal
Page House
39-41 Parker Street
London WC2B 5LH
Tel: 071-831 2000   **Fax:** 071-831 2223
Contact: Simon Anderson

Subsidiary Offices:

Bennetts Court
Bennetts Hill
Birmingham B2 5ST
Tel: 021-643 6255
Contact: Wendy Christiansen

Leigh House
28-32 St Paul's Street
Leeds LS1 2PX
Tel: 0532-450212
Contact: Katrina Smith

Imperial Building
Victoria Street
Nottingham NG1 2EX
Tel: 0602-483480
Contact: Barrie Fairbairn

Offices Abroad:

10 rue Jean Goujou
75008 Paris
France
Contact: Frédéric Foucard

Law Personnel

Personnel Management Consultancy to the Legal Profession

Professionalism at its highest.

Contact: Mack Dinshaw (Managing Director)
Stephen Watkins (Director)

Law Personnel
95 Aldwych
London WC2B 4JF

Tel: 071-242 1281   **Fax:** 071-831 2901

Zarak Hay-at-Law

Services: Job specification, register search, advertising assignments, media selection, copywriting. **Full details** and terms of business are contained in our client brochure - available on request from Bob O'Dwyer.

Zarak Hay-at-Law
6 Broad Street Place
Blomfield Street
London EC2M 7JH

Tel: 071-588 9887   **Fax:** 071-588 1911

Contact: Bob O'Dwyer

BADENOCH & CLARK

Legal Locum Division

Our LEGAL LOCUM division works closely with our permanent division and is well established in the expanding area of locum and contract recruitment. Locums provide clients with an additional option for cost effective staff resourcing — essential in today's competitive world of human resource management. Our locum division can deal with appointments, both short and longer term, in all areas of legal practice.

We are able to supply candidates (Solicitors, Barristers and Legal Executives) at all levels of qualification and in all areas of specialisation.

We can also supply temporary legal accountants, cashiers, cost draftsmen, outdoor clerks and paralegals.

Contact: **Helen Pearson, 16-18 New Bridge Street, London EC4V 6AU.**
Tel (071) 583 0073. Fax (071) 353 3908.

Simon Drake, Aqua House, 24 Old Steine, Brighton, BN1 1EL.
Tel (0273) 571490. Fax (0273) 571495.

Joe Reilly, Neville House, 14 Waterloo Street, Birmingham B2 5TX.
Tel (021) 631 4211. Fax (021) 643 7305.

BADENOCH & CLARK
recruitment specialists

Appendix B

Universities with Single or Joint Honours Degrees in Law (England and Wales)

Aberystwyth
Faculty of Law, Hugh Owen Building, University College of Wales, Aberystwyth, Dyfed SY23 3DY
(0970 623111)

Birmingham
Faculty of Law, The University of Birmingham, PO Box 363, Edgbaston, Birmingham B15 2TT
(021) 414 3344

Bristol
Faculty of Law, Wills Memorial Building, University of Bristol, Bristol BS8 1RJ
(0272) 303030

Brunel
Department of Law, Faculty of Social Sciences, Brunel University, Uxbridge, Middlesex UB8 3PH
(0895) 56461

Buckingham
School of Law, University of Buckingham, Buckingham MK18 1EG
(0282) 814080

Cambridge
The Faculty Board of Law, Old Syndics Building, Cambridge
University, Mill Lane, Cambridge CB2 1RX
(0223) 332350

Cardiff
Cardiff Law School, University of Wales, College of Cardiff,
PO Box 427, Cardiff CF1 1XD
(0222) 874000

City
Law Department, City University, Northampton Square, London
EC1V 0HB
(071) 253 4399

Durham
Faculty of Law, University of Durham, 50 North Bailey, Durham
City
(091) 3742000

East Anglia
School of Law, University of East Anglia, University Plain,
Norwich NR4 7TJ
(0603) 56161

Essex
School of Law, University of Essex, Wivenhoe Park, Colchester,
Essex CO4 3SQ
(0206) 873333

Exeter
Faculty of Law, University of Exeter, Amory Building, Rennes
Drive, Exeter EX4 4RJ
(0392) 263263

Hull
School of Law, University of Hull, Hull HU6 7RX
(0482) 465857

Keele
Department of Law, The University of Keele, Keele ST5 5BG
(0782) 621111

Kent at Canterbury
Department of Law, University of Kent, Canterbury CT2 7NP
(0227) 764000

Lancaster
Department of Law, Lonsdale College, University of Lancaster,
Lancaster LA1 4YN
(0524) 65201

Leeds
Faculty of Law, The University, Leeds LS2 9JT
(0532) 335033

Leicester
Faculty of Law, The University, Leicester LE1 7RH
(0533) 522363

Liverpool
Faculty of Law, The University, PO Box 147, Liverpool L69 3BX
(051) 709 6022

London:
King's College, Faculty of Laws, King's College, Strand, London
WC2R 2LS
(071) 836 5454
LSE, Department of Law, London School of Economics and
Political Science, Houghton Street, London WC2A 2AE
(071) 405 7686
Queen Mary and Westfield, Faculty of Laws, Queen Mary and
Westfield, 339 Mile End Road, London E1 4NS
(071) 975 5555
School of Oriental and African Studies, Department of Law,
School of Oriental and African Studies, Malet Street, London
WC1E 7HP
(071) 637 2388
University College, London, Faculty of Laws, University
College, London, 4–8 Endsleigh Gardens, London WC1H 0EG
(071) 387 7050

Manchester
Faculty of Law, The University of Manchester, Manchester
M13 9PL
(061) 275 3560

Newcastle
Faculty of Law, The University, Windsor Terrace,
Newcastle-upon-Tyne NE1 7RU
(091) 232 8511

Nottingham
Department of Law, The University, Nottingham NG7 2RD
(0602) 484848

Oxford
The Law Faculty Office, St Cross Building, St Cross Road,
Oxford OX1 3UR
(0865) 271490

Reading
Department of Law, Old Whiteknights House, University of
Reading, Whiteknights, Reading RG6 2AH
(0734) 875123

Sheffield
Faculty of Law, The University, Crookesmoor Building, Conduit
Road, Sheffield S10 1FL
(0742) 868555

Southampton
Faculty of Law, The University, Southampton SO9 5NH
(0703) 559122

Surrey
Department of International and Linguistic Studies, University of
Surrey, Guildford, Surrey GU2 5XH

Sussex
School of European Studies, University of Sussex, Falmer, Sussex
BN1 9QN
(0273) 606755

Warwick
School of Law, The University of Warwick, Coventry CV4 7AL
(0203) 523076

Polytechnics and Other Higher Education Institutions offering Full Time Law Degrees (England and Wales)

Anglia Higher Education College
Department of Law, Anglia Higher Education College, Victoria Road South, Chelmsford, Essex CM1 1LL
(0245) 493131

Birmingham Polytechnic
Department of Law, Birmingham Polytechnic, Perry Barr, Birmingham B42 2SU
(021) 331 5000

Bournemouth Polytechnic
Department of Law, Bournemouth Polytechnic, Poole House, Talbot Campus, Fern Barrow, Bournemouth, Dorset BH12 5BB
(0202) 524111

Bristol Polytechnic
Department of Law, Bristol Polytechnic, Coldharbour Lane, Frenchay, Bristol, Avon BS16 1QY
(0272) 656261

City of London Polytechnic
Department of Law, 84 Moorgate, London EC2M 6SQ
(071) 283 1030

Coventry Polytechnic
Department of Legal Studies, Coventry Polytechnic, Priory Street, Coventry CV1 5FB
(0203) 631313

Ealing College of Higher Education
Law Department, Ealing College of Higher Education, St Mary's Road, Ealing, London W5 5RF
(081) 579 4111

Appendix B 117

Hatfield Polytechnic
Department of Law, College Lane, Hatfield, Hertfordshire
AL10 9AB
(0707) 279000

Huddersfield Polytechnic
Law Department, Queensgate, Huddersfield, West Yorkshire
HD1 3DH
(0484) 422288

Kingston Polytechnic
Department of Law, Kingston Polytechnic,
Kingston-upon-Thames, Surrey KT2 7LB
(081) 549 1141

Lancashire Polytechnic
Department of Law, Lancashire Polytechnic, Preston, Lancashire
PR1 2TQ
(0772) 201201

Leeds Polytechnic
Law School, Leeds Polytechnic, Vernon Road, Leeds LS1 3EQ
(0532) 832600

Leicester Polytechnic
Department of Law, Leicester Polytechnic, PO Box 143, Leicester
LE1 9BH
(0533) 551551

Liverpool Polytechnic
School of Law, Social Work and Policy, Liverpool Polytechnic,
98 Mount Pleasant, Liverpool L3 5UZ
(051) 207 3581

Manchester Polytechnic
Department of Law, Manchester Polytechnic, John Dalton
Building, Chester Street, Manchester M1 5GD
(061) 247 2000

Middlesex Polytechnic
Department of Law, Middlesex Polytechnic, The Borroughs,
London NW4 4BT
(081) 202 6546

Newcastle-upon-Tyne Polytechnic
Department of Law, Newcastle-upon-Tyne Polytechnic, City Precinct, Newcastle-upon-Tyne NE1 8ST
(091) 232 6002

Nottingham Polytechnic
Department of Law, Nottingham Polytechnic, Burton Street, Nottingham NG1 4BU
(0602) 418418

Polytechnic of East London
Law Department, Polytechnic of East London, Barking Precinct, Longbridge Road, Dagenham Road, Essex RM8 2AS
(081) 590 7722

Polytechnic of North London
Department of Law, Polytechnic of North London, Ladbroke House, 62–66 Highbury Grove, London N5 2AD
(071) 607 2789

Polytechnic of Wales
Department of Law and Finance, Polytechnic of Wales, Treforest, Mid Glamorgan CF37 1DL

Sheffield City Polytechnic
Financial Studies and Law Department, Sheffield City Polytechnic, Pond Street, Sheffield S1 1WB
(0742) 533702

South Bank Polytechnic
Department of Law and Government, South Bank Polytechnic, 103 Borough Road, London SE1 0AA

Staffordshire Polytechnic
Department of Law, Cadman Building, Staffordshire Polytechnic, College Road, Stoke-on-Trent ST4 2DE
(0782) 412515

Wolverhampton Polytechnic
School of Legal Studies, Arthur Storer Building, Wolverhampton Polytechnic, Molineux Street, Wolverhampton WV1 1SB
(0902) 321058

Appendix B 119

In addition, a number of private colleges offer tuition for London University external law degrees.

The Careers Services Handbook for Solicitors is also recommended as an excellent source of useful information on law courses, and is available from the Central Services Unit, Armstrong House, Oxford Road, Manchester M1 7ED. This regularly updated guide sets out details of the relevant careers contact in the teaching institutions.

Appendix C

Code of Practice for the Recruitment of Trainee Solicitors

As agreed by the Association of Graduate Careers Advisory Services (AGCAS), the Association of Graduate Recruiters, the National Union of Students, the Law Society of England and Wales and the Trainee Solicitors Group.

This Code, first agreed in 1985, is under review at the time of going to press, and is likely to be amended into a new Guide to Good Practice in the Recruitment of Trainee Solicitors during 1991.

(1) No interviewing programme for the recruitment of applicants should be initiated before 1st September in the student's final year of degree studies.

(This is not designed to stop correspondence between firms and enquirers nor does it prevent visits by students to firms' offices either to gain vacation experience or to help them to learn more about the work of solicitors. It does, however, mean that no firms should before 1st September initiate any organised selection process, or follow up any 'presentation' made earlier in the year, wherever it took place.)

(2) Where representatives of firms of solicitors visit universities or polytechnics to interview applicants, such visits should not start before the beginning of the October term and dates of proposed visits should be agreed in advance with the appropriate careers service in each case.

(3) Ideally, an offer of articles to an undergraduate should not be subject to a time limit for acceptance. If, however, such an offer has to be made requiring a decision by a final date or specifying a date by which the offer, if not accepted, will be

Appendix C 121

deemed to be declined, that date should not be before 1st November in the final year or the expiry date of three weeks after the offer is sent, whichever is the later. (In the opinion of careers advisers, many students will accept offers before these deadlines. The rule should help firms who have been known to lose good candidates by pressing them for early answers. It should also be noted that it refers to undergraduates; the three-week rule is not intended to be applied to those who have already graduated.)

(4) Students will be expected to acknowledge within a day or two the receipt of any offer and if they are able to give immediately a final acceptance or rejection then they should do so. It will, however, be open for a student when acknowledging receipt to indicate that he or she wishes to have time to consider the offer and to state the date by which it is anticipated that a final decision can be given. If such a date is outside the time limit prescribed in the offer, the firm concerned should give sympathetic consideration to extending the time limit accordingly.

(5) Students will be expected not to accumulate offers. Offers should be dealt with as promptly as possible and students should restrict the number of outstanding offers held at any one time to no more than two. Once a student has accepted any offer, he or she should inform all other employers to whom applications have been sent and thereafter should make no further applications.

Index

'A' levels 24
Ability tests 49
ACAS Disciplinary Code 95
Accidents book 80

Bonus scheme
 for introductions 30

Cancellation of articles 65
Careers fairs 23
Commission for Racial Equality 30, 80
Common Professional Examinations 23, 25
Consistency
 importance of 2, 94, 103
Contract letter 16

Defamation 59
Demographic trough 4, 26

Exit interviews 13

Graphology 55
Group behaviour 72

Halo effect 50
Headhunting 33
Horns effect 50
Human resources plan 2

Injuries, reporting of 79
Inland Revenue 79
Institute of Legal Executives 8
Internal audit 3

Job descriptions 15, 68
Job evaluation 11

Listening skills 43

Mature applicants 24
Media packs 34
Milkround interviewing 23
Motivation 72

Office manual 7, 63

Para-legals 26
Person specifications 16
Personality tests 49

Quality of service 5
Questioning skills 43

Recruitment crisis 20
Rehabilitation of offenders 60
Resignations 3
Retirements 3

Statutory sick pay 79

Training 27, 39, 79, 88

Women solicitors 21

Young Solicitors Group 21